Democracy and Power
in New Zealand

For M

Democracy and Power in New Zealand

a study of New Zealand politics

Second Edition

Richard Mulgan

Auckland

Oxford University Press

Melbourne   Oxford   New York

Oxford University Press

Oxford   New York   Toronto
Delhi   Bombay   Calcutta   Madras   Karachi
Petaling Jaya   Singapore   Hong Kong   Tokyo
Nairobi   Dar Es Salaam   Cape Town
Melbourne   Auckland
and associates in
Berlin and Ibadan

First published 1984
Second edition published 1989
©Richard Mulgan 1984, 1989

ISBN 0 12 558200 4 second edition
(ISBN 0 19 558106 7 first edition)

Printed in Hong Kong
Published by Oxford University Press,
1A Matai Road, Greenlane, Auckland, New Zealand

Contents

Preface

Political theory is inescapable. All communities require some mechanism for making decisions which are binding on their members, and larger communities or nations all depend on permanent, elaborate institutions for this purpose. Politics, the activity concerned with these institutions of government, is, like any other area of social life, impregnated with theory, that is with general ideas about such matters as what governments ought and ought not to do, how politicians behave, the rights of citizens and so on. Much of this theorizing is unconscious, implicit only in the meaning of everyday terms, such as 'government', 'politician', 'citizen', in the routine procedures followed by those engaged in the practice of government or in the expectations which others may have of them. Sometimes these ideas are given more self-conscious expression, for instance in correspondence in newspapers or in the manifestos of political parties. Political theory as an academic enterprise concerned with formal and connected arguments about politics and political behaviour aims at still greater self-consciousness. It attempts to make more explicit what is normally implicit, to make more coherent what is normally incoherent and to examine critically what is normally taken for granted. Most of us do this to some extent; political theorists merely set out to be more formal, self-conscious and self-critical about politics than their fellow citizens, in order to help them and themselves understand politics more clearly.

Little formal political theory has been written about New Zealand politics. Our small size and limited resources, together with our close historical links with British political institutions and the western political tradition in general, have allowed us to depend on overseas writers and experience. Our analyses of parliament tend to be taken from Britain, our political sociology from the United States. Moreover, if there has been a dominant theoretical attitude in New Zealand political life, it has been that formal political theory is not to be trusted and that practical political experience is to be preferred to intellectual ideas or doctrines. This so-called 'pragmatism', the view that 'theory' is

7

dangerous — a view which is itself, of course, also a theory — has encouraged New Zealanders to think that they need not concern themselves too closely with articulating or criticizing the dominant principles and assumptions which underlie their political system. Yet, though we may agree that certain political ideas and doctrines, such as liberalism, conservatism or socialism, should not be followed in an extreme or doctrinaire form, this suspicion should not be allowed to extend to all ideas as such. To pretend that ideas are unimportant and that only facts matter is to overlook one of the most basic of political facts, that all political behaviour is informed, if only subconsciously, by ideas and beliefs. There is still much that we can learn from analyzing and reflecting on our political system, particularly if it is seen, for once, not as an offshoot or variant of other political systems but as an independent system worthy of study on its own terms.

The topic chosen is 'democracy', perhaps the central term in our political vocabulary. The term is first analyzed in the light of current New Zealand usage, and then a model or standard of democratic government is proposed against which the extent of democracy in New Zealand politics can be assessed. Various aspects of political practice are then compared with the model, and the study ends with a consideration of the main arguments for and against democracy. A great deal of ground is covered, at what may seem an alarming height of generality and speculation. Some important aspects of the political system are only briefly touched on or omitted entirely; but the partiality of treatment, the focusing on certain practices and institutions as particularly significant, is deliberate and may serve both to clarify discussion and to provoke argument.

Grateful acknowledgement is due to Betty Larkins and Jeannie Snow for patient typing and retyping; to Bernadette Thakur for research assistance; to Robert Chapman, Geoffrey Debnam, Paul Harris, John Morrow and the readers of the Oxford University Press for constructive comments on earlier drafts; above all, to Antony Wood who befriended a latecomer to the study of New Zealand politics and has throughout been unstintingly generous with information, criticism and encouragement.

8

Preface to the second edition

For this second edition, factual details have been revised, new examples added, and the bibliography brought up to date to cover the six-year period since the first edition was completed. In recognition of the growing awareness of the importance of biculturalism, a new section on democracy and Maori values has been added to chapter 2 and the material on the Maori seats in chapter 3 has been expanded into a separate section. A new section on interest groups and deregulation has been added to chapter 4. The overall argument and the model of democratic government have been left unchanged, although, in one or two respects, as will be made clear, the Labour government first elected in 1984 has been less close to the model than its predecessors, both Labour and National. Whether these variations represent permanent changes or are merely temporary deviations remains to be seen.

ONE: The meaning of 'democracy'

'Democracy': everyday usage

'Democracy' is a loaded, indeed an overloaded, word. It represents a powerful appeal to our fundamental political values and yet, through tired and self-serving repetition, it so often seems no more than vacuous rhetoric, empty of any real substance. We might, in despair, be tempted to abandon it altogether and search for newer, less tarnished terms in which to describe our political ideals. But this would be merely to dodge the problem, not solve it. 'Democracy' is a term embedded in our thinking about politics. Its meaning is blurred and contested precisely because our political thought inevitably involves debate and disagreement, and 'democracy' is one of the battlegrounds. It is too important to be ignored or replaced; we must instead make the effort to try to understand it.

In trying to penetrate the meaning of 'democracy' for New Zealanders, the more usual course would be to begin outside New Zealand. We could turn to the ancient Greek embedded in the word's etymology and arrive at 'people's (*demos*) power (*kratia*)'. Or we could quote one of the traditional formulations of democracy in English, of which the most famous is probably that of Abraham Lincoln in the Gettysburg Address — 'government of the people, by the people, for the people'. Or, again, we could look to the more recent past, to the revised definitions provided by political scientists, the most widely quoted of which is Joseph Schumpeter's — 'the democratic method is that institutional arrangement for arriving at political decisions in which individuals acquire the power to decide by means of a competitive struggle for the people's vote.'*

But though New Zealand democracy is part of a tradition which began many centuries ago on the other side of the world, we will

---

*Joseph A. Schumpeter *Capitalism, Socialism and Democracy* (London, 4th edition, 1952) 269.

not attempt to trace this historical development or to fix New Zealand's place within the tradition of western democracy. Our focus is more immediate and contemporary, directed towards the principles and practice of democracy in modern New Zealand. It is more appropriate, therefore, to begin our study of the meaning of 'democracy' by attempting to discover what meaning it has for modern New Zealanders. This approach may not lead to a radically different definition, but it will at least allow us to examine New Zealand usage with fewer preconceptions. Though the ultimate destination may be the same, the difference in route may prove instructive.

How is this to be done? One method which will immediately suggest itself to the political scientist is to ask people questions as part of a public opinion survey. A series of questions could be drawn up to test people's understanding of the word. For example, one could describe different types of government and political action, and then ask respondents whether or not they would call them 'democratic'. But there are good reasons for doubting whether this type of survey would provide reliable information, at least in this particular case. The decision to use the concept of democracy would be forced upon respondents by the interviewer, and they would be made to use the term in a context in which they might not use it of their own initiative. Moreover, with a term like 'democracy', which is so loaded with overtones of political debate and propaganda, respondents may be more influenced by what they think the interviewer wants to hear than by what they would normally say themselves. It is much better to look for instances where the user of the term is not aware that he or she is being investigated, and where the usage is therefore not contaminated by any desire to avoid offending the investigator.

The best available source of such spontaneous usage is written evidence, either an accurate record of the spoken word or written communication, such as an article or letter. In the quotations which follow, the main source of oral usage is the record of parliamentary debates in *Hansard*; other written evidence is drawn from newspapers, particularly letters to the editor, together with occasional quotations from editorial columns. Such evidence cannot be said to represent a properly random sample, as could be achieved with a public opinion survey, and is therefore not subject to statistical analysis. But it is at least restricted to spontaneous uses of the word and, particularly in the case of letters to the editor, may be said to represent a wide range of New Zealand usage of the term 'democracy' and its cognate adjective 'democratic' (italics mine).

1. The right of the people to decide their own future in a proper *democratic* manner should never be destroyed for the sake of expediency . . . the people would truly have their say and that is what we must give them in a *democracy*. (*New Zealand Parliamentary Debates* 394.4351 (18 September 1974))
2. If legislation vitally affecting any group in our society is to be brought in the Government should consult that group. That is a *democratic* concept. (*NZPD* 444.1268 (21 July 1982))
3. In this country we operate by majority rule, by *democracy*, and the National Government is determined that *democracy* will work in industrial relations. (*NZPD* 408.4125 (23 November 1976))
4. What I dislike . . . are minority groups who even after the taking of opinion and votes in an open and fair manner, still ignore the majority. Let us uphold the *democratic* principle we so often talk about. (Letter in *NZ Herald* 8 September 1975)
5. In a *democracy* such as New Zealand, South-Africa baiters like the minority group HART . . . have every right to express their opinions. (Letter in *The Press* 6 April 1980)
6. The essence of *democracy* is tolerance and understanding of opposition . . . in a real *democracy* everyone is entitled to speak his mind without fear. . . . (Letter in *NZ Herald* 26 May 1980)
7. It seems to me that the very essence of *democracy* is getting the maximum number of people to the polls to record their vote and so determine the Government of the country. The fewer the inhibiting factors, the better *democracy* is served. (*NZPD* 396.746 (22 April 1975))
8. Neither . . . can point to a black African nation where there is a *democratic* vote. There are dictatorships, rule by military cliques or tribal rule. *Democracy*, as practised in New Zealand, is unknown in black Africa. (Letter in *NZ Herald* 31 May 1975)
9. In the interests of *democracy* in New Zealand the number and size of the electoral districts for the North and South Islands and the Maori people too should be determined on the same basis. . . . (*NZPD* 397.1188 (20 May 1975))
10. . . . the essence of the word *democracy* is 'individual right to choose'. (Letter in *NZ Herald* 28 May 1980)
11. The Employers Federation aims to compel all employers to join its organisation, thus destroying *democracy*, the free enterprise system, the freedom of the individual. . . . (Letter in *The Press* 13 November 1974)
12. In a *democracy*, it is everyone's right to speak as they feel, without being criticised and accused: [let] freedom of speech prevail. (Letter in *Otago Daily Times* 10 June 1978)
13. . . . information is the currency of *democracy*. Accordingly, its undue suppression for the convenience or protection of officialdom devalues *democracy* itself. (Editorial in *NZ Herald* 2 August 1980)

We may make the following generalizations about the contemporary meaning of 'democracy':

(i)   it is the type of government which is generally claimed to be practised in New Zealand; for instance (in addition to 3, 5 and 8 above),

14. How can educationists on the one hand teach us that New Zealand is a completely *democratic* country and then on the other hand try to take away our right to choose our own education system? (Letter in *NZ Herald* 21 November 1975)

> (ii)   it is contrasted with dictatorship and authoritarian government; for instance (in addition to 8 above),

15. A sign of the vitality of a *democracy* is the presence of a wide diversity of pressure groups raising critical questions. The attempt to eliminate these groups . . . leads only to totalitarian centralisation of power. (Letter in *The Press* 16 February 1980)

16. *Democracy* is not an easy system to operate. In the name of freedom of speech, it permits hostile creeds to canvass for support in a way that would be unthinkable in authoritarian countries. (Editorial in *NZ Herald* 30 December 1975)

> (iii)   it is a form of government where all the people should have a say or be consulted, particularly in decisions which affect them; for instance (in addition to 1 and 2 above),

17. It is obvious that many age beneficiaries do not like the change which is to be made in paying their benefits. Why should the Government not be *democratic* and ask them? (Letter in *NZ Herald* 18 March 1975)

18. The essence of *democracy* is participation – by all. (Letter in *NZ Herald* 22 August 1980)

> (iv)   it involves the principle that when opinions are divided, the majority should prevail; for instance (in addition to 3 and 4 above),

19. The silent majority could then have the Government govern in the true *democratic* way, i.e. majority vote rule. (Letter in *The Press* 28 November 1974)

> (v)   it also involves the protection of minority rights; for instance (in addition to 5 and 6 above),

20. It is a basic tenet of this country's law and of *democratic* government that minorities who suffer injustice, whether real or imagined, have the right to be heard. (*NZPD* 394.4350 (18 September 1974))

> (vi)   it is particularly associated with the institution of voting at elections; for instance (in addition to 7 and 8 above),

21. People are often advised not to waste their votes on a third party. But

this is a *democratic* country and each of us has the privilege of expressing a preference through the ballot box. (Letter in *NZ Herald* 9 March 1981)

(vii) it involves equality of influence for each individual; for instance (in addition to 9 above),

22. I am not suggesting for one moment that the Maori voter, the Scottish voter, the Irish voter, and the Cook Islander voter who is eligible because he is here in New Zealand — should not have votes of equal strength. That surely is what *democracy* is all about. (*NZPD* 998.2199 (19 June 1975))

(viii) it involves freedom of choice; for instance (in addition to 10 and 11 above),

23. We are asked to believe that this is a *democratic* country offering freedom of choice. (Letter in *NZ Herald* 10 April 1974)

(ix) it involves certain particular freedoms, such as freedom of speech and opinion and freedom of information; for instance (in addition to 4,5,6 and 9 above),

24. The right to uphold unfounded, provocative and divisive opinions . . . is the great strength of *democracy*. (Letter in *NZ Herald* 25 February 1980)

25. Surely in *democracy* the ratepayer has the right to know what his council plans to spend his money on. (Letter in *NZ Herald* 30 September 1975)

(x) in general, as the overall sample of quotations indicates, it is often used to suggest approval of the government or institution so described; everyone is assumed to be in favour of democracy.

We may therefore sum up the commonly accepted conception of democracy in contemporary New Zealand as follows: it is the type of government which exists, or is supposed to exist, in New Zealand and is generally valued; under this type of government, the people have an equal say in decisions that affect them, and an equal say in electing those who exercise political authority; the principle of majority rule prevails though not at the expense of the rights of minorities; democracy is closely connected with the principles of equality and freedom, especially freedom of speech and freedom of information.

But such a conception, or set of conceptions, though adequate for everyday political discourse, should not satisfy the serious student of politics. There are certain ambiguities and inconsistencies which need to be removed if we are to engage in clear analysis and critical discussion about democracy in New Zealand. Such a process of refining and clarifying a term in ordinary language necessarily involves departing from the authority of usage. We become engaged in linguistic legislation, in prescribing what a certain word is to mean. There are obvious dangers in such a procedure. If, in our desire to operate with precise terminology, we stray too far from everyday usage, we may end up talking to ourselves — talking, it is true, in precise and even elegant terms, but in a way that is remote from most people's understanding or concerns. There would, in fact, be little point in using the word 'democracy'; we would do better to adopt an entirely new terminology to signify the fact that we were proposing a new and specialized style of discourse. Such specialized language has its place, in the social as well as the natural sciences, but it does carry the price of excluding the non-specialist. In the case of democracy, which normally implies that everyone should have a share, it appears particularly inappropriate to adopt a highly specialized and exclusive vocabulary. We will therefore look for a definition of democracy which is at once sufficiently coherent and consistent to serve as a basis for reasoned analysis and argument, and also sufficiently close to ordinary usage to be recognized as a refined version of the accepted conception of democracy rather than a wholly new concept.

A definition of 'democracy'

The process of refinement may begin with our noticing an important ambiguity in the everyday conception of democracy: the term is used to refer both to a form of political regime, typically one where the government is elected, and also to a particular method of making political decisions, where all the people have a say. We may describe these as the restricted and unrestricted conceptions of democracy, depending on the degree to which the people exercise political power or influence. Under the restricted conception, when we say that a community is democratic, all we usually mean is that the people have chosen their government and have the right to re-elect or replace it at regular intervals. For a regime to qualify as democratic in this sense, a limited role for the people is sufficient, extending only to the periodic choice of a government through free elections. In this restricted sense, we may say that New Zealand is a democracy whereas South Africa and China are not. Under the unrestricted conception, however, where democracy refers generally to political power exercised by the people, the focus is widened to include not just the way a government is chosen but the whole range of political decisions and governmental control within a community. The people's role is not confined to choosing a government; all political decisions may be made in a 'democratic' manner, that is with each person having an equal say in making them.

As a general definition of democracy, the restricted conception of democracy is open to a number of objections The particular criterion usually chosen, the existence of free elections, is too narrow. For instance, it concentrates exclusively on representative or 'indirect' democracy, where the people choose representatives to make decisions for them; it excludes methods by which the people may make political decisions directly, such as in public meetings or through referendums. Government by citizen assembly may not be practicable in most modern societies, at least at the level of national government; but referendums are not unknown in modern western societies and new electronic technology may make other forms of public decision-making increasingly possible. Moreover, apart from these methods of direct decision-making, there are other methods by which the people may influence government action, such as through the pressure of public opinion or lobbying by interest groups. Such indirect influences, as we shall see, are important democratic supplements to the electoral process but they cannot be counted as democratic features if democracy is defined solely in terms of elections. A more serious objection to any restricted definition of democracy is that it rules out, by definition, the possibility of increasing the level of democracy in a community beyond the particular minimum chosen. Once the minimum has been achieved, the community is fully democratic and cannot be made more democratic by extending the degree of popular power or influence. Not surprisingly, such definitions have been criticized as ideologically biased. Because democracy is usually assumed to be the best form of government, a restricted definition has the effect of recommending a restricted political role for the ordinary citizen.

An unrestricted definition, on the other hand, faces the charge of impracticability. If democracy is identified with a method of decision-making in which all the people share equally, then a true democracy has never existed and probably never could exist. The need for a social division of labour whereby different people perform different functions, quite apart from individual differences in political ability and inclination, makes a certain degree of political inequality inevitable. However, this is not a serious difficulty if democracy is seen not as an existing form of government, but as a tendency which actual governments may exhibit to a greater or lesser extent. A pure democracy where all citizens have equal power would be one extreme, an imagined limit, which existing regimes would approach to a greater or lesser extent. It would be what social scientists call an 'ideal type', meaning

17

not that it is ideally desirable but that it is an abstract construction, existing only in the imagination. In effect, the unrestricted definition identifies democracy not with a type of government but with a type of power distribution, which a political system may display to a greater or lesser degree. All political systems provide the people with *some* degree of political power, however limited, and are therefore democratic to a certain extent. The question of whether or not a political system is to count as a democracy becomes an irrelevant, or at least a secondary, question, a matter of deciding on some arbitrary cutting point on a democratic scale.

A restricted conception of democracy may still be of use in international and comparative politics, if we wish to distinguish between those countries where governments are elected and those where they are not. But in a study confined to politics within New Zealand it is less relevant. We want to see not whether New Zealand is a democracy, which it would be on almost any restricted criterion, but rather in what respects it is a democracy and whether it could or should become more (or less) democratic. For such questions the wider and more flexible definition is essential. For the purpose of this study, then, democracy will be defined as 'the exercise of political power by the people', taking 'power' in a wide sense to cover all means by which a person may affect the behaviour of others, including those relationships more commonly described as 'influence' or 'authority'.

This definition, too, may not be entirely free of ideological bias. Just as a restricted definition suggests a preference for a restricted role for the people, an unrestricted definition may be seen as biased in favour of extending the people's power as much as possible. The emotive and favourable connotations of the term 'democracy' make the act of defining it tantamount to a recommendation about how much political power the ordinary citizen should exercise. Those who wish to restrict the power of the people will choose a restricted or minimum definition of democracy; those who wish to increase it will prefer a more open-ended or inclusive definition. The value of democracy is so embedded in our ways of thought that declaring opposition to it has become shocking or at least paradoxical. Anyone wishing to criticize a government or procedure which others call 'democratic' is likely to deny that it is 'truly democratic' and will prefer to describe it in alternative terms, such as 'totalitarian' or 'anarchic'. However, if we are to think clearly and critically about democracy, we must try to get beyond slogans and be prepared to admit, at least as a logical possibility, that democracy and democratic procedures may be either good or bad. It should be possible to argue, for instance, that a further extension of popular power would be an extension of democracy, and still leave open the question of whether or not such an extension would be desirable. Thus, we may support an unrestricted conception of democracy as a term of analysis, because it includes a wider range of popular political power; but we are not thereby committed to advocating the maximizing of popular power.

Our proposed definition includes the main principles usually associated with democracy. For instance, it is closely linked to the principle of equality. When we talk of a decision being made by any group, we imply that all members of that group share in the making of the decision. If some members of the group exercise a disproportionate influence on the making of the decision, we are likely to say that the decision was not really made by the group as a whole but was, at least in part, the decision of a smaller, inner group. In other words, the notion of group decision-making implies the notion of equal sharing of power between the members of the particular group. In the case of the particular group which is the people, the principle of equality applies not only within the group but also to the composition of the group itself. 'The people' includes, or ought to include, everyone equally and without distinction. Indeed it could be argued that the principle of equality is the basic, defining principle of democracy, because, once it is accepted, we are committed to extending power equally to all and are therefore committed to democracy. When we look at the extent of democracy in a political system we are in fact looking at the extent of political equality in that system and the terms 'democracy', 'popular power' and 'political equality' may be used interchangeably.

Political equality is achieved if everyone contributes equally to the making of a decision, and the final outcome is one which everyone supports. But in many cases a satisfactory consensus may not be possible. Here, political equality requires that, if opinions are divided and a decision must be made, the view of the majority should prevail; to decide according to the wishes of a minority against a majority is to allow the members of the minority a disproportionate or unequal say. The principle of majority rule is thus also covered by our proposed definition, because it is a logical consequence of political equality.

Equality does not, however, give unrestricted rights to majorities. Though it may require that a given majority view be preferred to an opposing minority view, it may also require that further options be sought or compromises made which will give more people a more equal share of what they want. Political equality is primarily achieved by unanimity and consensus, and majority rule should be looked on as the democratic procedure of last, rather than first, resort. It does

19

not give majorities an unlimited license to rule in their own interest. Moreover, if equality implies that the final decision goes to the majority rather than the minority, it also implies that everyone's voice should be heard and their views counted. Any diminution of these rights, even by a majority, constitutes an infringement of democratic principles. Democracy, through the principle of equality, therefore implies the protection of individual and minority rights, which we have seen to be an important part of the contemporary conception of democracy.

Even where fundamental democratic rights are not at issue, democratic equality is infringed when certain groups or individuals are persistently outvoted by majorities. Though people who find themselves in a defeated minority on any one issue cannot claim to have been unfairly treated so long as their opinions have been sought and their votes counted, people who are consistently on the losing side on all or most issues may begin to feel less influential than those in a dominant majority. Political equality may thus require that, where the principle of majority rule is used, each person should have an equal chance of being in the majority; those who win today should lose tomorrow and vice versa. Democracy implies power sharing, which is not achieved if there are persistent, entrenched majorities and minorities. Thus, although the majority principle is fundamental to democratic procedures of decision-making, democracy does not countenance majority rule in the sense of domination by a particular majority over the rest of the population.

Not all minority rights are covered by the proposed definition of democracy. Consider private education. Some people claim that everyone has a right to freedom of choice in education and that minority groups, such as members of particular religions or social classes, should be allowed to establish schools exclusively for their own members. Others may oppose such a right on the ground that all children should have the same educational opportunities and should therefore attend similar schools. If the latter view prevailed and private education were banned it might be quite appropriate to say that individual freedom or minority rights had been curtailed. But would the action be undemocratic? It would, according to popular usage, which often equates democracy and individual freedom; but, according to our definition, there would be no breach of democratic principle so long as everyone, including the members of the minority groups concerned, had an equal say in arriving at the decision to restrict these freedoms.

In other words, democracy and democratic rights, according to our definition, refer to a particular type of procedure for making political decisions regardless of the content of such decisions; any decision may count as a democratic decision so long as it has been reached in a democratic manner. A possible exception is where a decision democratically taken, reduces or undermines the actual operation of democratic procedures themselves. For instance, a decision to deprive a certain minority of the vote, though it could be arrived at quite democratically, might be considered an undemocratic decision in that it would diminish the extent of political equality in the community. For the sake of consistency, however, it is better to describe such a decision as a democratic decision which will reduce the extent of democracy, or as an anti-democratic decision, rather than as an undemocratic decision.

Restricting democracy in this way to certain methods or procedures means that we must qualify the common identification or close association of democracy and freedom. Certain individual rights and freedoms admittedly are essentially connected with democracy. Such rights as the right to vote, the right of free speech, the right of free association or of forming organizations aimed at influencing government, the right of access to government information, must be guaranteed to all citizens if the people are to be able to exercise effective political power. Abridgement of these rights or freedoms is a curtailment of democracy itself. They may therefore be described as 'democratic' rights or freedoms. But there are other individual freedoms which, though commonly found in democracies, are not necessarily connected with democratic government. To take our earlier example, the right to private education is not obviously a democratic right, unless a case could be made for seeing the existence of private schools as necessary for promoting variety of thought and freedom of speech. Other freedoms, such as the freedom to open a shop on a Sunday or to opt out of a trade union, are even more clearly unconnected with the principles of democracy. It is possible to be against Sunday trading or in favour of compulsory unionism without compromising support for democracy, as it is being defined here.

Another way of making the same point is to distinguish between liberal government, that is government which is strictly limited in the extent to which it controls the lives of its citizens, and democratic government, understood as government in which the citizens share political power. 'Liberal democracy' may be a convenient slogan but it should be seen as a combination of two different, though over-lapping, sets of political values. There is no logical compulsion for liberal governments to be democratic or for democratic governments to be liberal, beyond the safeguarding of specifically democratic rights. We can readily imagine — and history may provide examples — extremely undemocratic and autocratic rulers who may yet exercise their power in a restrained and liberal fashion, preserving the lives and property of their citizens and protecting their civil and legal rights. Conversely a regime may be relatively democratic in its distribution of power and yet encroach very considerably on the personal freedom of its individual members. Indeed, during the last hundred years the extent of government regulation of the lives of individuals has increased at the same time as the extent of democracy has increased. Liberalism and democracy have not advanced hand in hand; rather, extension of the franchise helped to bring about the decline of nineteenth-century *laissez-faire* liberalism, not just in the economic sphere but also in the wider area of social welfare. The more influence the average citizen had over government activity, the more pressure there was on governments to provide for their citizens' wants.

This is another point at which political preferences may affect the choice of a definition of democracy. The main reason for separating liberalism from democracy is a desire for logical clarity: no disparagement of liberal principles is intended. However, someone who is particularly attached to liberal principles might disagree with our restriction and insist that all liberal principles should be included in the definition of democracy. As we have seen, the everyday meaning of democracy is wide and imprecise and any attempt to construct a clear definition must involve some departure from usage. The question then arises, which parts of usage are to be retained and which rejected. It is at this point that the evaluative tug of democracy may be too strong to resist. Anyone who claims to be offering a completely neutral definition of democracy may be guilty of self-deception.

Our proposed definition of democracy, as political power exercised by the people, covers most of the uses of the term in everyday usage. The discussion that follows should therefore be not too far removed from what New Zealanders ordinarily understand as democracy, and may thus contribute to our appreciation of the tradition of democratic government in New Zealand. In the interests of clarity, we have had to modify everyday usage in three respects — democracy is not strictly speaking a type of government but rather a type of power distribution which is found in different political systems to differing extents; democracy includes certain rights or freedoms which are essential to the exercise of popular power but excludes other rights and freedoms which may be demanded by liberal principles but not by democratic principles; 'democracy' is to be as far as possible a term of neutral value, referring to a particular type of political power without necessarily implying approval or disapproval. These modifications or refinements are necessary to avoid confusion but they still preserve a central core of the everyday meaning of democracy.

Who are 'the people'?

Though we may have decided on a definition, we have by no means dealt with all the problems involved in the concept of democracy. In particular, we need to consider certain difficulties associated with two key terms in our definition, 'the people' and 'power', both of which are far from transparently clear in meaning. In the first place, 'the people' is obviously a term of considerable ambiguity. This is not just because of variation in specific qualifications required for, say, registration as a voter in a particular district. At what age are individual members of the population considered sufficiently responsible to qualify for the vote? How long a period of residence is necessary before a person becomes entitled to participate in an election? These are important questions, requiring administrative rules and decisions, but they are not the most important problems associated with identifying the people. More fundamental is the question of defining the general population from which the people should be drawn to make a democratic decision on any given issue or set of issues.

For instance, on issues which affect New Zealand as a whole, say issues of national defence, the people are the qualified members of the population of New Zealand. However, if, when the Australian colonies were being united into a federal commonwealth, the New Zealand government of the time had accepted the offer to join the Australian states in a federal commonwealth, the 'people' concerned would be drawn from the whole population of Australasia and not just from the population of New Zealand. Indeed, on the issue of national defence in which both Australia and New Zealand have a shared and virtually identical interest, one could argue that the combined population of Australia and New Zealand is the logical group to decide, if questions of defence are to be decided democratically. National boundaries, in the sense of what defines a people united under an independent government, are often partly determined by historical accident. They may reflect a considerable unity of interest among their inhabitants, but there are always some issues which should more properly be decided by a larger or smaller 'people' than that defined by the existing national boundaries. Where these arguments become widespread and evenly balanced, they may develop into serious and often intractable political disagreements about national identity such as the conflict between Quebec and the rest of Canada or the troubles in Northern Ireland.

In New Zealand we may assume that the question of national boundaries, of what constitutes the New Zealand people, has been successfully settled for the time being. Dispute still surrounds the historical legitimacy of British settlement and the manner in which the Maori people were dispossessed of their land and autonomy. Whatever recompense may be due to the Maori for injustices past and present, almost everyone agrees that the present inhabitants of New Zealand are here to stay and are all legitimate citizens of the New Zealand nation. In the context of biculturalism, that is the coexistence of both Maori and Pakeha culture in New Zealand, some may not wish to refer to a single New Zealand people, a notion associated with the discredited policy of assimilation and integration of Maori and Pakeha. If the Maori people are to retain their cultural identity, we may prefer to speak of one nation with two peoples rather than one people. In our definition of democracy, therefore, 'the people' is to be understood to include all the citizens of New Zealand treated equally without necessarily implying cultural identity between them. Biculturalism, as we shall see, is by no means incompatible with democracy; indeed, democratic principles may be its best defence.

Even though we may agree who the people of New Zealand are, this does not solve all the difficulties in determining who are the proper people to decide democratically on any particular issue. On national questions, which affect everyone, there may be no problem: everyone should decide. But what about issues which affect only a fraction of the people? Where the issue is locally confined, such as a drainage scheme or a children's playground for those living in a particular area, should the decision be one for all New Zealanders or only for the people of that locality? In general, the decision should be left to those whose interests are affected by it. Otherwise, if all New Zealanders were allowed a say on all matters there would be no logical reason to stop at national boundaries: it would be equally consistent to require that everyone should have a say on everything anywhere in the world, a conclusion which is surely absurd. Each issue has its proper constituency, the group of people whose interests are affected by it. Because some issues are purely local in extent, a system of local government can be seen as an important supplement to a framework of democratic government. There are other issues which do not affect all New Zealanders but which are sectional rather than local in character, involving, for example, the interests and activities of members of a particular occupation, or those who participate in a particular sport or recreation.

24

Here the democratic solution would be to consult the members of the groups concerned. Thus, interest groups also become important adjuncts to democracy.

Allowing that different issues have different constituencies implies what is known as a 'pluralist' view of society. According to such a view, a society like New Zealand is divided into a plurality of different social groups, local, occupational, recreational, religious and so on, each with its own shared interests and patterns of social interaction. The memberships of these different social groups need not be mutually exclusive but may overlap: the same individual person may belong to a number of different groups, such as his or her family, locality, institution of employment, trade union, sports club or church. Local and sectional groups, however, are not the only social groups in any society. Each of us also belongs to the wider society or people as a whole, and will also therefore share in a collective or public interest as, for example, consumers or general members of the public.

Within such a pluralist society, some issues, as we have suggested, may affect only the members of a particular group; these may properly be left to the members of that group to decide. Often, however, the interests of one group in a society will overlap or conflict with those of another, and the members of more than one group will be involved. Moreover, if the general welfare is affected and the issue involves the expenditure of public funds, then the interests of the public as a whole are also affected. A typical example might be the issue of controlling the level of killing charges at freezing works. This will involve a clash of interests between farmers who will wish to reduce production costs and freezing companies who must remain profitable; freezing companies themselves will be divided between management, more concerned about their profits, and workers anxious to maximize their wages; the public as a whole will be involved because the prosperity of all depends on the proceeds of meat exports.

How are we to decide who has an interest in any issue? The notion of interests is very important in democratic theory and has been the subject of considerable philosophical and ideological debate. The view taken in this study will be that a person's interests are what is good or beneficial for that person. We have many different interests in the different aspects of our lives but, in each case, our interest is what is good or beneficial for us in that respect, as human beings, consumers, employees, parents and so on. How do we decide what is good or beneficial for each person? It will be assumed (a point to which we will return in the last chapter) that each person is the best judge of his or her own good and therefore of what his or her interests are.

On this view, the best way of arriving at the proper democratic constituency for an issue would appear to be to let individuals decide for themselves which issues they wish to take up. If the political system provides equality of political opportunity, then the appropriate constituency will emerge as a result of each person's choosing to take up matters which concern his or her interests and neglecting those which do not.

However, this method is not infallible. Apart from the practical difficulties of securing equality of political opportunity (which will be discussed in later chapters) there may be a principled objection to allowing individuals to have a say on anything they wish to. Suppose someone lives in a city and has no direct occupational interest in the freezing industry, but has a passionate hatred of freezing workers and is willing to spend a large part of his political resources on defeating the demands of the freezing workers' union. To the objection that it is none of his business, he replies that it is the only matter he really cares about and it has therefore become his business. He demands a vote in a ballot of freezing workers and insists on presenting his case to the minister of labour. We would not think it right that these requests be granted. Such a person, though he may be passionately concerned about the freezing industry, does not have what would be recognized as a legitimate interest in it (beyond the general interest he shares with all other members of the public).

Thus, the test of whether a person's interests are sufficiently affected to justify having a say in that issue cannot always be allowed to depend solely on the subjective views of the individual. An independent check on whether or not the interest is a legitimate one is required. Such a judgement will usually be in terms of whether the individual concerned has a material or financial interest at stake or whether the quality of his or her life may be directly affected. There will be room for dispute and argument about whether an interest is democratically legitimate or not. Should a self-constituted association of moral watch-dogs, such as the Society for the Promotion of Community Standards, have the right to a say in setting standards of censorship? Should an environmental organization, such as the Native Forests Action Council, regularly meet and lobby the minister of forests? In a reasonably democratic society, the question of the legitimacy of an interest will itself need to be settled in a democratic manner as a matter of public debate rather than by autocratic fiat. Individuals should be guaranteed the right to associate and have access to the media in order to press any cause they hold dear; those excluded from a decision should have the right to appeal to the public against their exclusion. This might seem to beg the question. If the question of democratic legitimacy should itself be settled by all members of society, what determines society's right to be the democratically legitimate group to determine the legitimacy of other groups? In practice, the national boundaries of a particular political system are taken as given; so too is the right of the society to decide issues within these boundaries. Our argument is that, if the society is a pluralist one, then only those individuals or groups whose legitimate interests are affected by an issue should decide that issue but that the people as a whole should be the final judges of which interests are legitimate.

The problem of 'intensity'

A further difficulty facing pluralist democracy concerns the weight to be given to each person's views in arriving at a democratic decision. If democracy involves political equality, each person, we may assume, will carry equal weight. Once the relevant constituency with the appropriate interest has been identified, it is then simply a matter of counting heads or votes. But what if different people can be affected to differing extents by the same issue? Such differences occur most noticeably with those decisions, common in a pluralist society, which involve the interests of different groups. In our previous example, it is plausible to see those who work in the freezing industry as having a larger stake in the question of killing charges because their livelihoods depend on employment in it; for farmers, on the other hand, killing charges are just one cost among many, though an important one; the ordinary citizen is involved even less. Should all whose interests are affected have an equal say or should they have a say in proportion to the degree to which their interests are affected? The position becomes even more complicated when we notice that there are similar differences not only between members of different groups, but also between different members of the same group. For one farmer, an increase in killing charges may be the last financial straw which drives him into bankruptcy; for another, it may make a hardly noticeable dent in a high standard of living. For one member of the public, a slight decrease in national prosperity may mean the difference between employment and unemployment; for another, its effect will be negligible. Are all these differences to be taken into account in assessing the extent to which the distribution of power in a community is democratic?

This problem is known in democratic theory as the problem of 'intensity'. We may imagine the analogy of three people planning to go out for the evening. Two would slightly prefer to go to a film than to a concert but are quite happy to go to either; the third prefers a concert and is most unwilling to go to a film. The normal solution among friends and equals would be to follow the preference of the stronger minority rather than that of the weaker majority. In politics, too, it is common for a government to pay more attention to a vocal minority than to an apathetic majority. However, the democratic principle of equality may require us to disregard differences of interest between members of the same constituency or people. For example, though some individuals stand to lose or gain more from a change in government after an election, we would not consider this any reason for revising the principle that each person's vote should count equally. Similarly, in the example of the two farmers or the two consumers differently affected by the same policy outcome, such differences do not justify differing degrees of influence, at least within a democratic framework. Indeed, in so far as the two individuals are members of a common constituency or community, they may be said to share the same interest as farmers or as consumers, and therefore to deserve the same degree of influence, as farmers or as consumers, though the personal consequences to each may differ.

On the other hand, particularly when we consider differences between reasonably well-defined groups rather than within them, the case for unequal influence becomes much stronger. This point is implicit in the example of the person obsessed with the freezing workers. We object to giving his views the same weight as those of the people immediately involved in the industry, even though he would have had some slight interest in it as a member of the general public. In a complex, pluralist society, people are often very remote from certain issues which still do concern them to some extent, for instance as consumers or taxpayers. It is not equitable to overlook all differences of immediacy and give all citizens an equal say, regardless of how close or how remote they may be. If the views of all who are affected are treated equally, the result will be to weight decisions overwhelmingly in favour of the larger, general interests, however dilute or distant they may be for each individual.

If differences of weight are to be allowed where different groups have differing degrees of interest in an issue, does this contradict the democratic principle of equality? It may be seen as compatible with democratic equality if that principle is broadened to include 'proportionate' equality, that is, an equality which allows each person a say which is equal in proportion to the degree to which his or her interests are affected. Overall, everyone's interests will still be given equal weight. Each person should have an equally large degree of influence over immediate issues, such as those affecting his or her locality or occupation, and an equally small degree over less immediate issues. In theory, the differences should be cancelled out and overall political equality maintained.

How are such differences to be assessed or measured? Intensity has often been considered a subjective quality, a measure of how strongly people feel about an issue; an intense minority is a group of people who are prepared to spend a great deal of political effort on an issue, raising funds, holding meetings, lobbying ministers and so on, in contrast to a majority who are largely apathetic and unwilling or unable to organize an effective opposition. However, if meat workers and farmers deserve a greater say in controlling killing charges than members of the general public, this is not simply because they feel more strongly or are prepared to organize more effectively to exert pressure. The reason is that their immediate interests, particularly their income and jobs, are more markedly affected by such charges. This would remain true even if they were politically apathetic and disorganized. If a wholly subjective criterion is adopted, it will once again allow the anti-freezing-worker fanatic who has little direct interest in the freezing industry to have a disproportionate influence on the meat industry.

The desire to involve oneself in business which may or may not be one's own cannot be counted as automatically justifying a greater share of democratic influence unless the degree of interest is a legitimate one. The question of how much influence any individual or group deserves cannot therefore be entirely left to the people concerned; we need an independent check. Again, because the final decision will often turn on factors which are imprecise or contentious, it cannot be left to a single unaccountable authority but must itself be subject to open debate and appeal.

In conclusion, then, democracy entails that all individual citizens should have a say in determining decisions in which they have a legitimate interest; where a number of people share the same interest, each will exercise the same degree of power; where different groups of people have different degrees of interest in an issue, the degree of power exercised by members of each group should vary accordingly.

'Power'

'Power' is perhaps the central concept in the study of politics but it is by no means unambiguous in meaning and has been the subject of much discussion and argument among political scientists. We need not follow these debates into all their intricate byways. None the less, if we choose to define democracy in terms of political power, we must at least be aware of some of the main difficulties and should clarify our position, even if without detailed argument, on some of the main controversies.

The focus of politics is government and political power is power over government and the manifold effects it has on the rest of society. The political sphere, it should be remembered, is not the only area of society in which power is exercised; each of the social groups in which we live, such as the family, the work-place, the local school or hospital, has its own power structure in which power can be distributed more or less equally. It is therefore quite appropriate to talk, for instance, of 'democracy in the home' or 'industrial democracy'; indeed, the degree to which democratic principles and procedures are followed in these non-political areas must have an important influence on the level of political democracy. However, in this study, we will be concentrating on political decision-making, the making of the numerous decisions which issue from the government and other political agencies; that is, we will be particularly interested in the power to make political decisions or to affect their content or timing. Such power must also include the ability to make 'non-decisions', that is, to prevent certain issues from ever reaching the political agenda. This form of power is often highly significant and can be overlooked if observation is directed only to those issues which are explicitly brought into the public arena.

Some scholars have objected to a concentration on decision-making on the ground that it is the eventual effect of government on society, political 'outcomes', rather than the formal process of government decision-making, which is crucial and which should be subjected to political analysis. This objection has force if there is a large gap between decisions and outcomes, if what is decided bears little relation to what actually happens. However, we will interpret the notion of decision-making widely, to cover not only decisions made at the highest level, for example in parliament or cabinet, but also the actions of officials and agencies responsible for administering government policy. Decision-making thus becomes the determination of government activity in all its aspects and the gap between decisions and outcomes is virtually eliminated.

Power, as the ability to affect decisions or non-decisions, can be exercised in a variety of ways, not all of which would ordinarily be associated with the word 'power'. In everyday speech 'power' is especially associated with force or coercion, as, for example, in the phrase 'naked power'. But we will be using it in a more inclusive sense. In a reasonably civilized political system, such as New Zealand's, political power does not often involve the open, or even implied, use of brute force. The sanctions are usually gentler, though no less effective for that; governments may be constrained, for example, by the possible loss of votes or of ministerial office, by personal embarrassment or by awkwardness arising from antagonizing people or groups with whom they must work closely. The ability to affect decisions in these ways is often described as 'influence' rather than 'power', but in this study will be included under the general heading of political power.

Also included will be certain instances of political decision-making which involve no sanctions at all, but where the wishes of certain groups are followed simply because of a belief that they should be. It is a well-observed fact of social control that certain individuals or groups have 'authority', by which may be understood the right to issue commands which are recognized as legitimate by the rest of the population. Obedience to such commands may follow simply from the belief that obedience is right and need not depend on the threat of any sanction. In the case of democracy, for example, a government may decide to follow public opinion on the ground that public opinion has authority and ought to be followed. Admittedly, in most cases, there may also be a sanction, such as the possible loss of votes. Still, such patterns of authority are, at the very least, a factor contributing to the distribution of power within a political system and therefore should be included in any account of political power. In what follows, then, we will be including what is usually described as 'authority' and 'influence' as well as 'power' under the general heading of political power.

Another problem, or rather set of problems, concerning the concept of political power is whether or not the exercise of political power need be conscious or deliberate. In the simplest, standard case of power, where A gets B to do or suffer something, it is assumed that A has acted consciously and deliberately and that B is aware of being made to act or suffer as a result of A's action. That is, both the 'wielder' and 'victim' of power are aware that power has been exercised. Democratic examples of this standard type of power are cases where decisions are directly determined by a public meeting, referendum or election. The people who make the decision are fully aware that they are making it. Those affected by the decision, for instance those who must implement it, also accept that a decision has been made. On the other hand, there are instances of the exercise of power, where one or other of the parties is unaware that power is being exercised. The wielder of power may influence other people without being aware of doing so. For example, a senior public servant, not wishing to offend a minister, may modify a course of action proposed by subordinate departmental officers and so make it more acceptable to the minister's point of view. This would be counted as an instance of ministerial power, even though the minister was not conscious of exercising any power.

Such cases are examples of 'anticipated reactions'; B expects that a certain action on his part will lead to a particular reaction from A which he wishes to avoid; he therefore 'anticipates' this reaction and avoids taking the original action which would have been likely to lead to it. In this way, A has affected the actions of B though he has done so unconsciously. Similarly, authority may be exercised without the knowledge of the possessor of authority. For example, politicians may be influenced by public opinion because they consider that they have an obligation to follow such opinion if it has been unambiguously expressed. Whether or not members of the public are aware that their opinion is having an effect on politicians does not alter the fact that it does have an effect. To discover the existence of such unconscious power, there is little point in observing or interviewing the wielders of the power because they are unaware that they are exercising it. Instead we must examine those over whom the power is exercised, and not just their external behaviour but the reasons why they have acted as they have. What we need to know is that B has acted out of fear of A's possible reactions or out of respect for A's authority.

The role of this hidden type of power, which does not involve the giving of any explicit commands or instructions, is important in any political system. It is particularly so in representative government where most of the power exercised by the people, it will be argued, is of this type. For instance, electoral defeat is a constant and powerful motive in politicians' minds and they are continually modifying their behaviour for fear of adverse public reaction and eventual loss of votes at the next election or in order to improve their public standing and therefore their electoral chances. The authority of public opinion may also play an important part in making politicians responsive to the views and preferences of ordinary citizens. The people may thus influence their elected representatives in a number of ways without being aware that they are doing so. This type of power may be exercised not only in actual political decisions but also in those non-decisions' where certain political issues or decisions are suppressed from the political arena through fear of adverse consequences which might follow if they were introduced.

Once this type of power is recognized, democracy is no longer confined, as it sometimes has been, to active participation by the people concerned. The people can also exercise power over decisions without taking any conscious or direct action. While spending most of their energies on other areas of their lives, such as their jobs and families, they may none the less exert a powerful influence over those more fully and professionally engaged in politics, provided that they retain the right to remove the politicians from office or otherwise make life uncomfortable for them if they become unresponsive to the people's wishes. That is, equality of power need not entail equality of active political participation but, in principle at least, is compatible with a political division of labour whereby some specialize in politics more than others.

So far we have required the existence of certain intentions or motives on the part of those involved in the power relationship: we have assumed an intention to exercise power on the part of the exerciser or wielder of power, as in the most straightforward, direct type of democratic power; or, as in the case of anticipated reactions or recognition of authority, where those wielding power may do so unconsciously, we have implied that those over whom power is exercised consciously recognize it. In both these cases, we can attribute power to those who possess it and thus attempt to assess how equally it is distributed. But the criticism can be made that we have left out certain aspects of social power which must crucially affect any assessment of its distribution. For instance, those who support a Marxist view of society and politics will take issue with a view of power which is restricted to conscious power. They will hold that the major fact about modern societies is the division into capitalists, who own the means of production, and the proletariat, who provide their labour under conditions enforced by the capitalists. According to this view of society, the political system is one of the instruments by which capital exerts control over society. Politicians and government officials may pursue the interests of capital without necessarily being aware that capitalists are exercising power over them. They may sincerely believe that everyone benefits when government intervention is kept to a minimum. Given an unequal distribution of economic power and political resources, however, this ideology will ensure that only the interests of the wealthy are protected by the state. Capitalists, too, may be unaware that they are using the state for their own ends. According to this analysis, the motives of participants are largely irrelevant. The main question is whose interests are served by the political system. If the interests of one particular group are served in preference to those of all others, then this group may be said to exercise overriding political power. Conversely, an equal or democratic distribution of political power will be indicated only by a political system which serves the interests of all citizens equally. This type of analysis is not confined to those who follow a strictly Marxist line; it is also adopted by those who stress the importance of 'structural' power, the capacity of social structures, such as the class system or the education system, to favour some and neglect others, regardless of the actual intentions or motives of any individuals who live within these institutions and in spite of political institutions which may formally extend equality of political opportunity to all citizens.

For this type of analysis the key factor is the final outcome of the political process. Those whose interests are favoured by certain institutions are identified as the people who exercise power through those institutions. Democracy or political equality thus becomes the equal satisfaction of each person's interests in so far as they are affected by government, regardless of who actually brings the result about. As we shall see, particularly when discussing the relative power of interest groups, the degree to which different groups benefit is often a good indication of how much power they wield. A group which is particularly well treated may turn out to be one wielding considerable influence which might otherwise go undetected. But receiving benefits from government is merely evidence from which the possible exercise of power may reasonably be inferred; it does not itself constitute power or necessarily entail its existence. We should leave open the logical possibility that a political system could be highly democratic in its distribution of power, and yet act in the interests of only one class or section of society.

Conversely, there could be a highly undemocratic government, such as a theocratic monarchy, which acted in the interests of all members of society, while keeping all political power in the hands of one person. Such governments, no doubt, have rarely, if ever existed; indeed, as we shall see, one of the major arguments for democracy over other political methods is that it is more likely to yield decisions which are in the interests of most people. But the possibility of such regimes should not be ruled out by definition as it is if democracy is identified with the effects of the political system, rather than with the processes by which these effects are brought about. As we stipulated earlier, democracy should refer to a particular method or methods by which decisions are made rather than to the nature or content of such decisions. The connection between government by the people and government for the people is best seen as a matter of observable fact rather than as true by definition.

Assessing equality

We have been referring throughout to 'equality' or 'the equal distribution of power' within the political system. These apparently simple terms conceal a very complex reality. In the first place, democracy and equality are matters of degree. Pure democracy or pure equality are practically impossible; in virtually every situation someone or some group will be more or less influential than others. The assessment of democratic power is thus a comparative question, concerned with determining greater or lesser degrees of equality or inequality.

Secondly, when talking of a greater or lesser degree of political equality, we are not implying that institutions or countries can be ranked on a single scale of equality, as one might rank, for instance, the tendency of sons to be of equal height to their fathers. Power is not a simple concept like height. In assessing the degree of equality we will have to look at a number of different variables, for instance the proportion of members involved in the decision, whether some of these people are more involved than others in spite of an identical degree of interest, how many are influential at each stage of the decision, and so on. Rather than say absolutely that one institution or procedure displays more equality of power than another, we must specify in what respect it is more equal. One institution or procedure may well be more equal than another in some respects and less equal in other respects. For example, ancient Athens was more democratic than New Zealand in the number of decisions that were taken by 'the people', but New Zealand is more democratic in who is counted as a member of 'the people'; neither state can therefore be said to be more democratic or less democratic without qualification, but both are more democratic and less democratic in different respects.

Thirdly, even if we concentrate on one particular dimension or variable, though we may be able to assess differing degrees of equality, we may not be able to reduce them to quantifiable figures. Some variables, such as electoral turnout, are readily quantifiable, but others, such as the degree of responsiveness of politicians to their electorates, are not. Here we may talk of 'more' or 'less' without being able to specify precisely how much more or how much less. Similarly, we may talk of giving the 'same weight' or 'less weight' to different people's views without being able literally to weigh them or assign them numerical weights. The mathematical implications of the notion of equality cannot always be applied literally. It does not follow, however, that assessments of equality or differences of power are wholly arbitrary, or that the attempt to assess degrees of democracy is hopelessly flawed. This would be to accept the quantifier's fallacy, the belief that what cannot be reduced 'to numerical precision is necessarily random and arbitrary, without any rational or reasonable basis. Though complete precision and certainty are unattainable, it is possible, when describing political power, to make reasonable judgements, based on ascertainable evidence.

TWO: A model of democratic government

The need for a model

Democracy has been defined as the exercise of political power by the people. The people consists of those whose legitimate interests are affected and who can be considered sufficiently responsible to decide for themselves. Each person is to have the same amount of power as everyone else with a similar interest. Where the interests of different groups are affected to differing extents, the degree of power exercised may vary in proportion, though not all differences between groups and individuals will be sufficient to justify a corresponding inequality in the distribution of power.

When we turn to the question of how democratic the distribution of power is in a particular political system such as New Zealand's, the quantity of possible evidence may appear overwhelming. Political power, as we have seen, is a highly complex relationship which exists in many different forms at many different levels of society. The casting of a vote at a general election, a caucus debate, a speech at a party conference, a meeting between a minister and interested parties, an MP's private calculation of political advantage, a letter to the editor — these are just a few examples of ways in which the people may exercise political power and there are countless others. To describe all these instances in detail would be tedious and ultimately confusing; we would have lost the wood in a myriad of trees. We need a means of organizing the mass of evidence so that it can be comprehended and evaluated. We need what social scientists call a 'model', that is a mental plan or picture of how a particular social institution works.

Though it has become a technical term, the term 'model' refers to a common feature of everyday experience. We all have such pictures or models of familiar social institutions, such as the family or the school. These involve certain assumptions about the purposes of the institutions (looking after children, education), their different members (parents, children, teachers, pupils) and the proper behaviour associated with each member. In politics, too, we all have views, often vague and ill-defined, about how parliament works or about the respective roles of the prime minister and the governor-general. The very activity of living in society and learning its language means that we acquire certain models or theories about how we and others should live. In this sense, we are all social theorists, though we may not know it. What distinguishes the models of the social scientist is merely that they are more precise and better articulated than those we share as average citizens.

In this chapter, a particular model of democratic government will be described in outline and defended as appropriate for a discussion of democracy in New Zealand. Any model will be selective; it will highlight some aspects of political behaviour and play down others. Being selective it will also be partial, urging a particular emphasis and point of view. The proposed model is no exception. It is closely based on New Zealand political practice, both past and present, though, as we shall see, it runs counter to some common views about the constitution. It will thus be partly descriptive, a means of understanding how the people exercise power in our system of government, but will also be frankly an exercise in persuasion, recommending that democracy in New Zealand be seen in this particular way.

Though the model follows in broad outline the institutional structure of contemporary New Zealand government, it does not assume that political equality actually exists in contemporary New Zealand. It is a model of democratic government in which political power is distributed equally among all the citizens, not a description or summary of contemporary New Zealand politics. The question of how much political equality there is in the New Zealand political system is left open and will be discussed in the following three chapters when contemporary political practice will be compared with the various aspects of the model. Though the model is a standard of democratic government, an 'ideal type' of democracy in which political equality is maximized, it is not to be understood as ideal in the sense of a best form of government. It may provide the best approach to the problem of how the people are to exercise power in a society like New Zealand, and may therefore be more appropriate for New Zealanders than some other democratic models. But it is not meant as an ideal blueprint of how the New Zealand political system should best be organized. As we saw, democracy is merely the name for political equality; such equality is not necessarily valuable to the exclusion of all other values or to be maximized at all costs. There may be other values which would be compromised if we attempted to come as close as possible to the model. What these values might be and whether they justify limits to the desirability of the model are questions which will be raised in the final chapter.

The model outlined

The essential characteristics of the model are simply described. The people are to exercise power through three major sets of institutions. One is the parliamentary system whereby the electorate is offered a periodic choice between alternative party governments with alternative personnel, principles and policies. The main function of parliament is not to decide which party will govern — that properly is a decision for the electorate — but to provide a public forum for party competition. In parliament, the ruling party (or parties, in the event of a coalition) must seek public, legal endorsement for its policies and must therefore explain and defend its general conduct of business; opposition parties subject their opponents to continued scrutiny and try to present themselves to the public as alternative governments. The desire of all parties to maintain and increase their popularity with the electorate constrains the ruling party to act according to the wishes of the public. There are other means, besides party competition, by which the institution of parliament allows members of the public to influence government action. Individual MPs or groups of MPs for a particular region may act on behalf of constituents in a non-partisan manner; in parliamentary committees, party conflict may be forgotten and consensus achieved. But party competition is always present potentially, and the regular appeal to the electorate remains the mainspring of parliamentary democracy.

Secondly, there is the interest group system. Round the government and the public service at every level are organised semi-public or private groups, variously described as 'interest groups' or 'pressure groups'. Their function is to articulate the interests which their members share on particular areas or questions of government policy, and to attempt to influence government in their direction. Some of these groups, such as Federated Farmers or the Manufacturers Association, are elaborate organizations with permanent offices and staff. They are consulted as a matter of course on a continuous series of issues. Others may be more ephemeral, created to support or oppose some particular measure and then disbanded. The authority of interest groups is in many cases publicly guaranteed by statutes which establish their powers and membership or which determine their right to be represented or consulted. Other groups are independent of the formal structure of government. All interest groups, however, share the common aim of trying to secure government action favourable to their interests.

Thirdly, there are the institutions of local government. Members of local communities share certain needs which are best provided for by local agencies, with the coercive authority of government to raise revenue and enforce compliance with local regulations. The various institutions of local government — general-purpose bodies, such as city, borough and county councils, and special-purpose bodies, such as catchment boards, harbour boards and electric power boards — allow members of each local community to share in controlling their own activities.

These three sets of institutions are closely connected with one another. The parliamentary and the interest group systems have the same focal point, the cabinet, those members of the ruling parliamentary party who are ministers in charge of government departments and who together form the most authoritative body in central government. Lower down there is also considerable interpenetration: interest groups try to influence the views of political parties and MPs as well as those of government departments, and MPs present the parties' views to sectional interests. Similarly, the institutions of local government interact with the parliamentary system, through contact with political parties and local MPs. Local bodies are also active within the interest group system, and have their own national associations competing for government attention alongside other interest groups. The three sets of institutions are intended to complement each other in ensuring that the different demands of different sections of the people are translated into political action. Some interests, such as sectional interests relating to particular economic or occupational groups, will usually work through the interest group system. More general interests, such as those of consumers, will rely more on the parliamentary system, which encourages politicians to appeal to the wider public. Individual and local interests are likely to make use of either the local government system or the parliamentary system. The guiding principle for the model is that set out in the previous chapter: all citizens are to have an equal share in determining the political decisions in which they have a legitimate interest.

In the rest of this chapter we will describe some general features of the model and some reasons why it is more appropriate for New Zealand than some other possible models of democracy. That the model closely follows the existing institutional structure of the New Zealand political system will already be clear; it can also be shown to incorporate a number of general assumptions and values which are well established in New Zealand social and political history.

A moderately pluralist society

In the first place, the model assumes what may be called a moderately pluralist view of society. Some models of democracy look only to the whole and require popular power to be exercised only by all the people taken together; they do not accept that popular power can or should be exercised by separate interests and groups. Such models treat society as if it were a single homogeneous community: they overlook or reject the division into different social groups and interests which is characteristic of most industrialized societies. Indeed, some more radical opponents of pluralism are prepared to reject industrial society altogether, and advocate small, simple communities or 'communes' in which there will be little need for social differentiation or sub-groups with separate, conflicting interests. On the other hand, proponents of more extreme forms of pluralism see the political system as merely an arena for competition between special interest groups. They assume that society is totally differentiated into sectional interests and that there is no overall unity or common interest, only an aggregate of groups and group interests.

In most relatively small or homogeneous societies, however, there is a considerable degree of community and common interest between all members of society. Fellow citizens may belong to a great variety of different local communities, occupations and other organizations, but they also share certain common, national concerns; there is thus a common or public interest as well as sectional or local interests. Such a society may therefore be characterized as moderately pluralist because its members' lives and interests are partly, but not wholly, differentiated into separate groups. The proposed model is appropriate for such a society because it allows the people to exercise power both through their various groups and sections and also as members of the public as a whole. There can be little doubt that New Zealand society is itself moderately pluralist and that, in this respect, the model fits New Zealand conditions.

Government as a specialized function

A second assumption of the model is that government is a specialized function of society, needing special institutions such as parliament, the public service, organized interest groups, local bodies and so on. There is a division of labour in politics, even in a democratic society, which requires that some people specialize and make a career in the business of government whereas others, probably the majority, take only an amateur interest in politics and participate only occasionally; in other words, there is a division in society between government and citizen.

This division is not hard and fast. There will be many on the border line, whose involvement in politics goes beyond that of the average citizen but who are not totally involved professionally in government. Leaders of major interest groups, for instance, may spend considerable time on political activity and may acquire considerable political experience, but they will usually retain employment in their respective occupations and will not be engaged full-time in politics. Some belong on both sides, for instance, members of the public service who are part of the government but, as private individuals, exercise the rights of ordinary citizens. None the less, in spite of these complications, it is still possible to made a broad distinction between the government and its citizens. The assumption that government is a specialized function is clearly entrenched in New Zealand life. From the beginning of European settlement it was taken for granted that political authority would be exercised by authorities, whether the colonial governor and his staff or an elected house of representatives.

A model which allows some people to participate in politics more than others might appear undemocratic on the ground that those who participate more will have more power. Indeed many democratic theorists have proposed models of democratic government where there is no difference between rulers and ruled, and where all citizens are equally involved in the political process. They have drawn their inspiration from communities like ancient Athens or the early colonial settlements in New England, where decisions could be taken by all, or most, male citizens, either meeting together or alternating in positions of responsibility. However, as we argued in the previous chapter, not all political power need be exercised directly or consciously. There is also the indirect, unconscious power of anticipated reactions where, for example, voters may exert power over elected officials without taking any deliberate steps to do so and even without being aware that they are having any influence. Apparent apathy or lack of overt participation is quite compatible with the exercise of this type of power. An individual or group may have a fair share of political power without actually participating beyond quite a minimal level. Indeed, lack of involvement may be evidence of satisfaction with the degree of responsiveness from government, whereas active participation may be a sign of dissatisfaction and of an inability to exercise power through the hidden rule of anticipated reactions. For this reason, then, democracy, defined as equality of power, need not necessarily entail a model of government in which all participate equally. The proposed model, which allows inequality of participation, can also count as a model of democratic government where, in principle at least, power can be exercised equally by all members of the community.

Not all abstention from political activity is necessarily evidence of indirect power; those who do not take part may simply lack the ability or resources to press their own interests adequately. Some democratic theorists have unfortunately blurred this distinction between the various possible reasons for abstention and have assumed all apathy to be evidence of political satisfaction. They have been charged with excessive optimism (or cynicism) in neglecting the actual inequities of contemporary society and in appearing to idealize the status quo. Such complacency is rightly to be rejected. But the insight that overt participation is not essential for the exercise of political power should not be discarded simply because some theorists have misused it. The proposed model does not make the mistake of assuming that people always abstain from a position of political strength rather than weakness; it is therefore not open to the charge of justifying an unequal distribution of political power and resources. Though it does not require equal political activity, it certainly assumes equal political power. Democratic equality is possible only if the less politically active are able in some way to constrain and control those who are more politically active. A relatively low level of overt participation in politics need not imply any corresponding lack of interest in politics. Someone who does not attend meetings or sign petitions may, through the media or in discussion with family, friends or colleagues, keep a close eye on the actions of those who do participate and indeed may be ready to participate if he or she considers it necessary. The taking of such an interest (or at least the belief among decision-makers that such an interest is being taken) is necessary for the effective exercise of indirect democratic power through anticipated reactions. An intelligent interest in politics of this private, secluded sort might even be regarded as a form of participation no less than the public participation favoured by participatory democrats.

Values supporting the model

If political equality is to be achieved without maximizing political participation for all, governments and decision-makers in general must be kept responsive to the wishes and demands of ordinary citizens. To help secure this responsiveness, the political system must incorporate certain values. One is a respect for each individual's democratic rights, such as the right to vote, the right to associate for political purposes with people of similar interests, and so on. Without these rights, individuals will not be able to exert pressure on government decisions, either directly, through voting for one political party or interest group representative rather than another, or indirectly, through the decision-maker's perception that they will withdraw their support or change their allegiance. Democratic rights are essential if alternative views are to get a hearing and if neglected groups and interests are to have a chance of influencing public policy. Governments or interest groups may not always want to protect everyone's democratic rights, particularly those of their political opponents. These rights must therefore be safeguarded by a commitment to their value which is seen to override anyone's immediate interest.

Democratic rights involve democratic duties. Each person must participate to the extent necessary to ensure that the political system responds to his or her demands. Personal self-interest will often be an insufficient motive for an individual to engage in political activity, even of the most minimal sort, such as voting or paying membership dues. In any large group, the chances that one individual's contribution will affect the outcome are minute and the benefit likely to be gained by participating will be much less than the personal cost of such participation. The purely selfish, calculating egoist will prefer a 'free ride' at the expense of others and will run the risk of his or her abstention making any difference to the final outcome. If everyone makes this calculation independently then no one will participate and the advantages which would have followed from concerted action will be lost. For this reason, even a democratic model which requires only a moderate degree of participation, will need to rely on more than self-interest as a motive for political action. Some notion of a moral obligation or duty to contribute to a common objective will also be required. Individuals must believe that, if others pay to help bring about a good which can benefit all members of their group, it is not morally right or fair for any one of them to refuse to contribute.

If citizens must accept a duty to participate in pursuit of the interests they share with each other, governments and politicians should also accept a duty to follow or anticipate the wishes of the people as a whole or of particular sections of the public. Responsiveness to the public will often be in the interests of governments seeking re-election or bound by constitutional procedure or convention. But such constraints may not always be sufficient to guarantee that a government pays attention to the public's wishes. They will also need to be supplemented by a commitment to the final authority of the people, the view, sometimes described as 'populism', that politicians and those in official positions ought wherever possible to follow the opinions and preferences of the ordinary citizen.

These various values, which are required by a model of democratic government with a high degree of political specialization, are all well established in New Zealand life. They may not be sufficiently observed to guarantee political equality in practice, but a model which incorporates them will be building on values which are widely supported. For instance, it is unquestionably part of the agreed core of political principles in New Zealand, that all adult members of the community, with one or two minor exceptions (such as recent immigrants, the insane, criminals convicted of serious offences), should have basic democratic rights, such as the rights of free speech and expression, the right to associate or form groups organized round any legitimate interest, the right to vote in free elections. These rights are listed in the United Nations Declaration of Human Rights as the essential political rights (Articles 19-21) and, particularly in the modern western tradition, are considered necessary for human freedom and self-respect. In New Zealand, democratic rights of voting are enshrined in the Electoral Act. This is the only Act of the New Zealand parliament containing entrenched clauses which cannot be amended in the normal way by a simple majority, and is therefore our closest approximation to a written constitution. Again, the origins of these principles are to be found in the attitudes of the early settlers who, as British colonists, claimed at least the same political rights as citizens of their home country. As a newspaper editor in the Bay of Islands asked in 1842:

Has anyone, even in the seat of Sovereignty, the power, constitutionally speaking, to deprive British subjects in any part of the world of their natural right to govern themselves? (*The Observer* 19 May 1842)*

Similarly, in the words of E. G. Wakefield, the leading spokesman of organized colonial settlement:

What is it [responsible government] but the practical recognition of the Colonist Class as equally entitled with the Metropolitan to the enjoyment of the inherent political and civil rights of the British subject; the treatment of the Colony, not as a mere appendage but as an integral part of the Empire? It gives the Colony so favoured free institutions as nearly as may be resembling those of the Mother Country, the political institutions which we have a right to take for granted they will prefer before any others that could be offered them.†

*Quoted by S. Cheyne *Search for a Constitution* (PhD thesis, University of Otago, 1975) 202

†M. F. Lloyd Pritchard (ed) The Collected Works of Edward Gibbon Wakefield (Glasgow and London, 1968) 73

Similar views were held by each succeeding generation of immigrants, with increasing confidence as voting rights became more widely established in Britain itself. To begin with, the franchise in New Zealand was restricted to property holders (though the level was low and not strictly enforced) and to males. By the end of the nineteenth century, however, the principle of equal voting rights for all adult citizens was firmly established. Though, as we shall see, there have been certain minor irregularities in the electoral system, the general principles of 'one person, one vote' and 'one vote, one value', have become unquestioned, fundamental assumptions of the political system.

It would also be generally accepted that the individual citizen has a duty to exercise his or her right to vote at both national and local elections. As we shall see, even in local elections where turnout is low, most voters accept that they ought to vote, whether or not they actually do so. The duty to vote is a familiar and entirely non-controversial theme of newspaper editorials on the eve of elections. For instance:

there is a strong obligation on everyone to cast a vote. Unless most electors exercise their franchise the results of the poll will not represent and might seriously misrepresent the opinions of the people. (*The Press* 29 November 1969)

Democratic responsibility requires all qualified voters to exercise their franchise today. Voting may be voluntary; it is a fundamental civic duty, none-the-less. (*NZ Herald* 14 July 1984)

In the various interest groups, each member is also regularly expected, as a matter of duty, to make some active contribution to the organization, at least in terms of formal membership and an annual subscription. On the other hand, there is little indication of a duty to exercise all the democratic rights to the fullest degree possible. Activities such as holding meetings, organizing petitions and so on are universal rights not duties. That is, citizens must not be prevented from performing them if they wish to, but they are not under an obligation to perform them or liable to blame if they do not. Whether individual citizens and rank and file members do in fact make a sufficient minimum contribution to ensure proper responsiveness from leaders will be discussed in later chapters. As we shall see, there are important areas in which the minimum is too low. None the less, there are certain sections of the community, such as farmers and doctors, who have exercised at least their fair share of power with only a moderate degree of active participation by the rank and file and a considerable degree of anticipated reactions. This suggests that the most fruitful approach to equalizing power in New Zealand is not through a model which maximizes participation for all, but through one which encourages the minimum degree of participation necessary to achieve responsiveness on the part of elected leaders.

Finally, the responsiveness to public wishes which the model requires of leaders is one which is closely matched by the style of leadership dominant in New Zealand politics. All governments appointed by genuine elections must pay at least some attention to popular demands. But in New Zealand this responsiveness has been particularly marked. From the early days of settlement, the government was often the only available source of capital and technical skill and was called on to help directly in the economic development of the country to an extent rare in most other Western countries. Correspondingly, a populist style of political leadership developed in which close attention was paid to the public opinion of the day. Seddon, the first long-serving political leader elected by universal franchise and still in many respects the archetypal New Zealand politician, was extremely sensitive to expressed and potential demands. As Sidney Webb, the English socialist, commented,

his dominant desire and most permanent impulse is to conduct the business of government so as to obtain the greatest advantage for the majority of the people, with the expectation that, if he does so, he will be kept in office . . . he is intensely responsive to any public opinion that can express itself in a majority of votes or even in a minority likely to prove dangerous to his continued supremacy. In America he would have made a first-rate machine politician. . . *

Similar comments were echoed by Seddon's contemporaries. His colleague and successor, Joseph Ward, wrote:

he had the true democratic conviction that it was his duty to give effect to what he believed to be the will of the people. Indeed, one of the great secrets of his success was that he possessed the gift, or knack, or whatever it may be called, of anticipating the trend of popular feeling; the happy gift of intuition.**

Sympathy with popular demands could be viewed more cynically as merely the desire for popularity and electoral success. In Seddon's own words, 'Keep the b-s on a string and then they'll keep you in office'.† But under our model, leaders are not required to be responsive to public opinion out of a disinterested conviction that the wishes of the people should be followed. Such high-minded motives should not be ruled out as impossible, but they are not essential to the model

*D. A. Hamer (ed) *The Webbs in New Zealand* (Wellington, 1974) 39,36
**James Drummond *The Life and Work of Richard John Seddon* (Christchurch, 1906) viii
† Quoted (*sic*) by Keith Sinclair *William Pember Reeves* (Oxford 1965) 225

which places more emphasis on the politicians' desire for electoral popularity as an incentive to anticipate the reactions of the electorate.

Corresponding to this attentiveness to popular demands has been a relative lack of interest in political or economic doctrine and a lack of concern for consistency of principle. 'Socialism without doctrine' was how a French observer described antipodean experiments in state intervention. 'Mr Seddon was not a theorist . . . [but] was always intensely practical' said an obituary notice.‡ The same combination of sensitivity to popular demands and flexibility of doctrine has been found in all subsequent political leaders who have achieved positions of dominance. For instance, William Massey, whose Reform Party succeeded the Liberals in office, was described by a contemporary in terms very similar to those applied to Seddon:

on all questions of political strategy and tactics Massey had a flair for knowing the trend of public opinion and what measures he could induce parliament to adopt. This instinctive, practical, empirical knowledge of what the man in the street thought, Massey had gained by long years of arduous fighting and constant direct contact with all classes of electors, both in town and country.§

The first Labour Prime Minister, Michael Joseph Savage, continued in this tradition. As his biographer has written:

Savage himself appreciated how far the people were willing to go and what they wanted most from the government. He showed this by playing down Labour's socialist past and emphasising that 'we intend to begin where Richard John Seddon and his colleagues left off.'**

John A. Lee, Savage's leading opponent within the Labour Party, paid unconscious tribute to this characteristic of Savage's when he said of him, 'He leads by following. Being unimaginative he has no sense of contemporaneity and advances with the common mean.'† The same style of leadership continued with the long-serving leaders of the National party, Keith Holyoake and Robert Muldoon. Mr (as he was then) Holyoake's sensitivity to public opinion was well known. In the words of a leader of the Labour opposition:

He was a politician of his times and he very accurately reflected the views of that time. Indeed, few politicians were better at reflecting those views. He could put his finger up and tell exactly which way the wind was blowing.‡

‡ *New Zealand Graphic* 27 June 1906
§ William Downie Stewart *Sir Francis H. D. Bell, His Life and Times* (Wellington, 1937) 11
**Barry Gustafson *Michael Joseph Savage* (Wellington, 1968) 59
† Quoted by Keith Sinclair *Walter Nash* (Auckland and Oxford, 1976) 108
‡ *N.Z. Listener* 8 March 1975, 18-19

Sir Robert Muldoon is a self-confessed admirer of Seddon§ and swept to power under a thoroughly Seddonian campaign slogan, 'New Zealand the way you want it.' David Lange is in the same mould, chosen and supported by his colleagues as a popular, entertaining leader who communicates sympathy with the concerns of the average voter. The government over which he presides may have been unusually doctrinaire in economic policy, but its vote-catching combination of right-wing economics with left-wing foreign policy and protection of trade unions from an even less sympathetic opposition may be seen as a new variation in populist opportunism.

The preference for popularity rather than principle, for pragmatism rather than doctrine, has always had its critics, particularly among those who have a more academic or theoretical interest in politics. Such people tend to place a high value on theoretical consistency and on self-conscious adherence to abstract political doctrine. At the same time they may have less time for the less well-articulated views of the ordinary voter. They have tended to criticize New Zealand politics as 'politics without ideas', and its politicians as opportunists who will adopt any course of action so long as it wins them votes. There has been a tendency to disparage the leaders who have trimmed their sails to suit the electorate and to sympathize more with the unsuccessful ideologues, men like Pember Reeves in Seddon's cabinet and Lee in the first Labour government (both, incidentally, fine and prolific writers).

Whatever one's political prejudices, however, leaders like Seddon, Massey, Savage, Holyoake and Muldoon have certainly won widespread support among both political colleagues and the electorate at large, and must represent the dominant tradition of political leadership in New Zealand. Their pragmatism, their willingness to sacrifice consistency for popularity, should not necessarily be seen as evidence of lack of principle or intellectual barrenness. The rejection of ideology in politics is itself ideological; it reflects a particular view of the priorities which governments ought to follow. It implies that what individual citizens think they want at any given time is more important than any abstract theory of what is good for them or of what they might want if they saw things differently. The opportunism of politicians need not be simply the cynical pursuit of votes, though this may often be their dominant motive. It may also be an endorsement of the final authority of the public's wishes. Where there is a clash between any theory of what people ought to want and what they actually want,

§ R. D. Muldoon *The Rise and Fall of a Young Turk* (Wellington, 1974) 7

preference is given to accommodating actual wants. Pragmatism is thus complementary to populism, the view that the opinions of the people should prevail, however distasteful or inconsistent they may seem to the élite few.

Democracy and Maori values

The Maori people and their political traditions have so far had little influence on the development of democratic government in New Zealand. Democracy is a product of the western, European tradition and its existence in New Zealand is due to European settlement and the subsequent dominance of those with European ancestry. Even the particular characteristics of New Zealand democracy which distinguish it from democracy in some other western societies, for instance its relative populism, are the result of factors within Pakeha New Zealand society rather than Maori society. Although some attempt has been made to incorporate a specifically Maori element, for example the Maori seats in parliament, the New Zealand Maori Council and the Waitangi tribunal, on the whole, from the traditional Maori perspective, the New Zealand political system appears overwhelmingly Pakeha and alien.

While the dominant goal in race relations in New Zealand was that the two races and cultures should become assimilated into a single, homogeneous society, the alien nature of the system of government could be seen as a temporary and passing feature. In due course, all New Zealanders, Maori and Pakeha, would feel equally at home in institutions which matched their common culture. However, the goal of assimilation has become increasingly discredited because it amounts to the destruction of Maori identity and values by the Pakeha majority. Instead, there is now much greater emphasis on biculturalism, the coexistence of two cultures, Maori and Pakeha, within one nation. In this context, the alien origin of democratic government becomes more problematic. How can the institutions of government be said to meet the needs of both cultures if they arise out of the traditions and values of only one of the cultures? Is the commitment to a model of democracy such as we have outlined another instance of Pakeha monoculturalism?

Although democracy is clearly European and Pakeha in origin, its values and procedures are not necessarily totally alien to Maori values and procedures. While there are clearly some important differences, there are some underlying similarities as well. Decision-making in

Maori culture centres on face-to-face discussion. At meetings on a marae, speakers put forward opposing points of view and after debate, often prolonged and interspersed with informal discussion, a consensus is reached. Every member of the local community (the tangata whenua) has the right to attend the meeting, though not all may have speaking rights — women are often not allowed to speak and sometimes only one person from each family, the respected elder (kaumatua), will speak. The use of public meetings and the free expression of opposing points of view have affinities with the small, community-based direct democracies of ancient Greece and colonial North America (where, incidentally, full membership was also denied to women).

Maori society also developed representative institutions where decision-making was delegated to leaders speaking on behalf of their own families or communities. Individual villages had their runanga, councils consisting of the kaumatua from each family meeting with the chief (rangatira). When the need arose to discuss issues on a broader front, particularly in dealing with the Pakeha, use was made of the wider runanga, a meeting attended by chiefs and elders from all the villages and tribes affected.

Leadership in Maori society was usually based on descent and seniority, but it was always subject to the continued support and consent of the people; chiefs and elders could be bypassed or replaced if they proved incompetent or disloyal. Contact with European culture and its changing technology has lessened the importance of accumulated experience and age as a criterion for leadership. Formal education and up-to-date skills have also become valuable and have opened the way for younger leaders to be given more influence in Maori decision-making. Thus, representative democracy, with its leaders responsible to the people who have chosen them, is in tune with the Maori approach to reaching decisions that involve relatively large numbers of people. So too is the distinctively New Zealand emphasis on populism, the responsiveness of political leaders to the values and attitudes of the average citizen. Maori leaders, although expected to have distinctive authority, are quickly criticized if they distance themselves too far from the concerns of people back home on the marae.

One apparent difference between democratic principles and Maori political values is the democratic emphasis on the formal equality of each individual and opposition to distinctions based on characteristics such as race, gender, or status. Traditional Maori society placed great emphasis on such distinctions, giving particular authority to the eldest born males in certain families and would certainly not have subscribed to the political equality of all adults. Yet the differences should not be exaggerated. On the Pakeha side, formal equality of political rights has coexisted with significant differences of political influence and participation according to class and gender. As far as modern Maori are concerned, the influence of Pakeha society has created a need for other types of leadership and experience, besides that of the local elders. Increasingly, too, Maori women are demanding and securing a position of equality on the marae. Because of large-scale migration and intermarriage, tribal distinctions have become more fluid, particularly in the cities, and there is a greater readiness to give all Maori people equal rights, whether or not they have ancestral links to the places where they now live. In these ways, Maori are themselves incorporating the principle of formal equality of political rights within their own values and procedures. Given that our model of democracy also requires political specialization and leadership, elements which remain integral to Maori politics, its assumption of equal political rights is not inconsistent with the survival of Maori political procedures.

A related, more general, respect in which democracy is sometimes said to be incompatible with Maori values is its supposed 'individualism', that is its emphasis on the importance of individuals treated separately, which contrasts with the importance Maori attach to their collective life in social groups, such as the extended family or the kinship-based village with its marae. This difference is sometimes expressed in terms of contrasting priorities: for the Pakeha (as for other westerners), the individual is prior to the group, whereas for the Maori (as for other members of tribal societies) the group is prior to the individual.

Again, although there are important differences of value and behaviour between Maori and Pakeha, such as the undoubted difference in family structure, these differences should not be overstated. We may readily concede that Pakeha society, like other western societies based on a capitalist economy, places more emphasis on individual rights and freedoms and on personal self-interest and self-development than does Maori society. Family relationships are more attentuated and the pursuit of individual self-interest more encouraged.

However, democracy as such does not necessarily imply a view of society in which individuals are seen as isolated, independent individuals. This view is more properly associated with one particular brand of democracy, sometimes called 'liberal democracy', the ideology which combines support for democratic rights with a stress on social and economic freedom and a limited role for government intervention. Contrasted with liberal democracy is 'social democracy', in which commitment to democracy is combined with support for a collective, public approach to social and economic organization. Thus, liberal democracy is the ideology of *laissez-faire* economics and the free market, while social democracy is the ideology of socialism and the welfare state. Both are equally legitimate branches of the democratic tradition. Though, liberal democracy may be the dominant ideology at present in western societies, New Zealand has been noted for its relative commitment to collective solutions and to the welfare state. To accommodate this tradition, our model of democracy is pluralist rather than individualist in its premises, seeing New Zealand society as made up of a number of different groups rather than individuals. Within this pluralist framework, there is no reason why one section of the population, the Maori people, should not organize themselves in a particularly collective and co-operative manner with greater emphasis on family and kinship relationships, provided only that each person within these groups achieves equal power. (Nor, incidentally, does such collectivism necessarily preclude economic advancement in a capitalist society. As the examples of the Japanese and overseas Chinese suggest, economic success can be based on group loyalties and strong kinship networks and does not require the individualism more characteristic of western societies.)

The aspect of democracy which is perhaps most frequently seen as destructive of Maori culture is the democratic emphasis on majority rule, the right of majorities to prevail over minorities. A contrast is sometimes drawn between the Pakeha method of counting votes and following the majority and the Maori method of reaching a consensus which requires everyone to agree with a decision. However, this difference may be a matter more of decision-making style and custom than of fundamental principle. Although Maori debates and discussions usually end with everyone agreeing on a particular course of action, the formal consensus does not necessarily mean that everyone agrees that the final decision is the best. Those who opposed it may have changed their minds; more usually, however, they will have seen that they are outweighed and will therefore formally concede defeat. In the same way, Pakeha meetings where differing points of view are expressed sometimes end with the person in the chair assessing the prevailing opinion which is then put to the meeting and accepted unopposed.

Whether or not a vote is taken, it is usually agreed that the majority view should prevail. The difference lies in the extent to which this agreement is articulated. This, in turn, depends on different social conventions about the significance of remaining silent. For the Pakeha, silence implies acquiescence; the losing minority accept their defeat without further discussion. For the Maori, on the other hand, silence implies continued opposition. To indicate acceptance of a decision to which one was originally opposed, one must publicly and explicitly endorse it. In each political culture, however, we can discern the same basic principles: the need for all views to be expressed; the value of finding a solution acceptable to all, that is a genuine consensus, if at all possible; if complete agreement is not always attainable, then the decision should go with the majority, provided always that the rights of the minority are not infringed. Although styles of decision-making differ and more formal votes are taken in Pakeha than in Maori institutions, neither culture has a monopoly on either consensus or majority decision-making.

A more serious objection to the majority principle is that it appears to countenance the subjection of the Maori people themselves within a society in which they are outnumbered. The Pakeha, having settled in the country in overwhelming numbers, legitimize their occupation with the democratic majority principle which conveniently allows them to oppress the indigenous minority. This, however, is a mistaken interpretation of democratic principles as we are understanding them. As we saw in the first chapter, the dominant principle of democracy is equality and the majority principle should not be allowed to override it. Democracy demands that the fundamental rights of everyone, including members of minorities, be upheld. It also, ideally, requires that all groups and individuals have an equal share in influencing political decisions and in having their interests met by government and its agencies. Where a particular group is consistently disadvantaged, the principle of equality can also be used to justify special remedial treatment, 'affirmative action' or 'reverse discrimination', on behalf of the disadvantaged. The majority principle is a method of reaching decisions which treats everyone's opinion equally. However, it operates democratically only where everyone has a chance of being in a majority and no minority is consistently on the losing side. Democracy does not license a majority to dominate or oppress a minority. Conversely, those who wish to preserve the rights of indigenous or other minorities are not licensed to overthrow democracy on the ground that it offers them no protection. On the contrary, it requires fair and equal treatment for all.

In general, we can agree that democracy is part of the western political tradition and that many of its procedures are, like other aspects of western culture, alien to traditional Maori values. There is no doubt that the Maori people and their culture are seriously threatened in contemporary New Zealand. The preponderant numbers of the Pakeha population, together with the pervasive power of the modern western-style economy, make their survival extremely difficult. The legitimacy of original settlement and the need to compensate the Maori people for injustices of the past are beyond the scope of this study. However, given the fact of European settlement and the need for Maori people to adapt and survive within a predominantly western society and economy, the values of our democratic model are not to be seen as an additional threat to their separate identity or survival. Both the equality and the pluralism of democracy are not so much the problem for the Maori people as an important part of the solution.

In this chapter we have outlined a model of democratic government which is pluralist and provides political equality without requiring either equality of political activity or a maximum of political participation. We have argued that it fits with certain assumptions and values well-established in New Zealand political life. In describing the model and defending it against various criticisms which have been made of pluralist theories of democracy, we have begun to articulate a justification of this type of democracy in terms of the values which underlie it. But this justification will not be fully developed until after we have compared the model with contemporary political practice. When we have been able to assess, if only in a general way, the extent to which New Zealand politics is democratic in terms of the model, we will be in a better position to consider what arguments can be offered in favour of this type of democracy. It should also be remembered that this model, though it may be ideally democratic by definition, is not necessarily ideal in the sense of being the best imaginable form of government for New Zealand or any other country. There may be countervailing values and arguments which can be used to justify limits to the pursuit of political equality. But these arguments, too, will be more clearly appreciated after we have examined the actual extent of political equality.

THREE: The parliamentary system

Parliament and political parties

Parliament, like any other durable and valued institution, has many functions. It embodies a public commitment to the rule of law and the accountability of government to the people; all statutes of law must pass through its procedures and all ministers are responsible to it. Its rituals and traditions symbolize the victories won by the British Commons in its struggles against the arbitrary power of the Crown, and then transferred to British settlements abroad. According to our model, its main function is to enable the electors to choose a government by voting for various parliamentary candidates offered by competing political parties. The central fact about parliament is that its members are divided among different political parties, with those belonging to the majority party forming the government and the others forming an alternative government or opposition, who hope themselves to become the government at the next election. Party is thus the dominating factor of parliamentary practice; it is the main qualification on which members are elected and it forms the motive power of most parliamentary action.

The centrality of party in parliament is not recognized in the constitutional theory which underlies the formal practice of parliament. The laws and regulations governing the conduct of elections and the legal procedures under which parliament conducts its business make very little reference to the existence of party identification or to party allegiance on the part of representatives. According to the strict letter of constitutional law, each electoral district or constituency elects an individual member to represent it. The assembly of all such members, the House of Representatives, then meets to enact legislation, approve the raising of revenues and the allocation of funds to various government departments. These departments are in the charge of ministers appointed by the Crown, that is the Queen's representative, the governor-general, not by parliament, though ministers are themselves MPs and are answerable to parliament for the conduct of government business.

None of this is false, but as a description of what happens, it is highly misleading. In every case, the reason why individual MPs are elected is that they stand as members of a particular party which aims to have enough members in the house to form a majority and thus become the government. Similarly, the ministers who form the cabinet and run the government are not effectively chosen by the governor-general. They are chosen first by the electorate which gives a party a majority in parliament, and then by the majority party in parliament from among its own members. There are slight differences of practice between the two parties. In the Labour party, ministers are formally elected by the parliamentary party. In the National party, the choice is officially left to the leader of the party, who becomes the prime minister if the party is successful at the polls. But the leader is himself elected by the parliamentary party and can be unseated at any time; he must therefore take careful note of his colleagues' wishes when choosing a cabinet. The existence of large, disciplined political parties thus enables an election to be a choice between different parliamentary teams, that is between alternative governments. Without party identification and party unity, the choice of government would be made not by the electorate on election day but, as was more common in the nineteenth century, within parliament itself by shifting coalitions of individual members and their factions.

We are assuming that one party wins sufficient seats to form a majority and that parliament is essentially a forum of competition between two parties, one the government and one the opposition or alternative government. The existence of minor parties is not ruled out altogether, but their main function is assumed to be parasitic on two-party competition. They act as repositories for protest voters who express displeasure with the major parties, and are thus a means of keeping the major parties sensitive to the wishes of the electorate. They do not, however, form part of either the government or the main opposition. The model is quite compatible with the rise of a new party, such as Labour in the 1920s and 1930s, or with an electoral coalition. Labour's opponents, the United and Reform parties, eventually joined together to become the National party but they might have remained distinct in coalition, like the Australian Liberal-National alliance which allows Australian federal politics to function in most respects as a two-party system. In such cases, the essential feature of the two-party model is that the party or group of parties which is to govern is chosen by the electorate at the election rather than by parliament after the election.

The official designation of an MP as an individual representative of a particular district without any reference to party allegiance is not altogether ill-founded or without purpose. Some of the functions of an MP are as a non-partisan spokesman for local interests. Furthermore, the formal emphasis on each member's status in his or her own right is important symbolically in upholding the independent authority of parliament as a whole or of individual members if they are threatened by the ruling party. Governing parties need to be reminded from time to time that they are not above the law and that they depend ultimately on the electorate, who choose to elect a parliament of party members but could choose otherwise. Constitutionally and morally, parties are the creatures of parliament and the electorate. None the less, the relative blindness of laws and formal rituals to the fact that the major function of an MP is to be part of a party team is dangerous. It helps to perpetuate the misapprehension that there is something constitutionally disreputable or undemocratic about political parties. As we shall see, the truth is quite otherwise. Political parties and the competition between them are an aid, not a hindrance, to democracy; attempts to weaken the dominance of parties are often attempts to lessen rather than increase popular influence over government.

The governing party and the pursuit of office

The governing party, chosen by the electorate, is the major medium of democratic control in the parliamentary system. By the governing party, in this context, we mean the parliamentary party or government caucus, consisting of those MPs who make up the cohesive, governing majority in parliament. A political party, of course, is more than just its parliamentary members. Members of the extra-parliamentary party, both the dues-paying members and the activists and officeholders, are also important, particularly for the selection of parliamentary candidates and the organization of election campaigns. But it is the parliamentary caucus itself which is the central focus of a party's power, especially when the party occupies the government benches.

The government caucus includes cabinet ministers, under-secretaries and backbenchers, a group of about fifty people, depending on the size of the party's majority. The size of the House of Representatives has been gradually increasing since 1969, under the provision that the number of South Island seats is fixed at twenty-five and the number of North Island seats is decided on a similar ratio of seats to population. With the total number of seats now ninety-seven, forty-nine is the minimum size of a governing caucus. The largest government caucus so far is that of the Labour government elected in 1987 which has fifty-seven members. The 1984-7 Labour caucus had fifty-six, while the 1972-5 Labour and the 1975-8 National caucuses each had fifty-five members. (These numbers include the speaker who, though usually not attending caucus, remains a government member.)

The caucus as a whole meets once a week when parliament is in session, and periodically at other times. There are also frequent meetings of caucus committees, sub-committees of caucus, when backbenchers may join with appropriate ministers to discuss particular proposals or specific areas of government activity. In addition to formal meetings, members of caucus are in continual contact with one another, both within and outside parliament. Caucus members see themselves as part of a team, dedicated to maintaining their superiority in the House and in the electorate. Because it is a team and because open dissension would present a damaging impression of disunited and ineffectual government, caucus tries always to present a unified stance to the public. Differences of opinion may exist within the party but the official caucus view, like the official cabinet view, is always a unified one – hence the secrecy and confidentiality which surround the details of caucus business.

How do the people exercise power through the governing party? We will assume that everything a party does in order to become or remain the government is an instance of the power of at least some part of the electorate. The fact that parties wish to secure the support of the voters and that voters are free to give or withhold their votes provides the voters with a sanction which can be used to influence the political parties. To win elections and become the government, political parties must tailor their behaviour in ways which will win them popular support; in doing so, they submit to constraints set by what they think the voters will approve or disapprove. Such influence is indirectly and unconsciously exercised by the voter in the form of reactions anticipated by the politicians. The evidence for it is found in the actions of politicians which follow from their desire to win, or their fear of losing, an election rather than in any direct instructions issued by members of the electorate to them. Without a desire to win on the part of parties and politicians, the individual voter's sanction of giving or withholding his or her vote would be ineffective. This aspect of democratic control thus depends on the self-seeking ambition of the politician.

Such an assumption of self-interest on the part of politicians may be offensive to some supporters of democracy. The democratic tradition is in part high-minded and idealistic, and it may seem discordant with this tradition to rely on the ambition of politicians rather than appeal to their sense of duty or public service. Certainly, political ambition must be tempered by integrity. Democratic competition between political opponents should be free and equal; those in power should not use their position to bend the administration of elections in their favour or unfairly damage the political opportunities of the opponents. For instance, ministers should not use information legitimately gathered by the police or the security service to discredit the reputation of a political opponent. The electoral sanction itself is not always sufficient to guarantee honest practice by politicians, particularly when their activities are hidden from the public view. We need to be able to rely at certain points on their personal integrity and their commitment to everyone's democratic rights. We must also accept that much of what politicians do is done with a sincere conviction that they are acting in the best interests of the community and not just from a calculation of electoral advantage. None the less it is deceptively easy for successful politicians to persuade themselves that what is best for them and their immediate circle is also best for the public in general. Politicians are not necessarily lacking in scruple or concern for others; but, like most of us, they are more likely to live up to their principles if it is in their own immediate interests to do so. It is thus a strength not a weakness in democracy that it harnesses the politician's ambition and desire for office to the pursuit of popularity.

If democracy requires politicians and political parties to solicit support and votes from the public, New Zealand is reasonably well-served. Both major political parties, on the whole, tailor their activities and programmes to appeal to the voters. Labour, however, has sometimes been less whole-hearted in the pursuit of power. The reason lies in the party's principles and *raison d'être*: it is in origin a programmatic party, established as the political wing of the labour movement to work for the achievement of certain social and economic goals. Admittedly, the aims of the party have been considerably revised since the party was founded in 1916; for instance, the original socialist programme was diluted in the late 1920s by the abandonment of the call for the nationalization of land, thus helping to make the party more acceptable to rural voters and paving the way for eventual victory in 1935. The latest reformulation of the socialist objective (1974) was merely 'to educate the public in the principles of democratic socialist and economic and social cooperation'. In the amalgam of humanitarian, egalitarian and co-operative ideals which make up the modern socialist tradition, Labour in New Zealand was nearer the moderate end of the spectrum, stressing gradual reform by constitutional means rather than revolutionary seizure of political power or the complete abolition of private property. Doctrinaire socialism obviously has been unpopular with the New Zealand electors, and Labour's moderation showed that the party was willing to adapt its policies in order to enhance its electoral prospects. None the less, the conflict and debate among party members which accompanied such adjustments revealed important tensions within the party. There were some Labour supporters who thought that the major goal was to work for a socialist future and who were reluctant to compromise long-term principles for the sake of short-term popularity; others, however, believed that any Labour government would be better than a National government and were prepared to adapt party policy in ways which were more likely to win support in the electorate. The latter, more pragmatic, view has tended to predominate within the parliamentary party and has usually prevailed among the majority at the annual conference, the party's main authority on matters of general policy. Under the Lange government, tension between the parliamentary and party supporters has increased as the government adopted neo-liberal principles which, in contrast to traditional socialism, seek to reduce, rather than enhance, the role of the state in economic and social policy.

The National party, on the other hand, has usually been less susceptible to such tension between doctrine and the pursuit of power. Not that it is without principles or values; it has consistently supported individual freedom and private enterprise and from time to time there have been clashes between the more and the less doctrinaire adherents of these principles. But such conflicts have been less frequent and less bruising than in the Labour party. The origin and overriding purpose of the National party has been not so much to enact a particular set of principles as to prevent the election of a 'socialist' government. The party was formed in 1936 as an anti-Labour coalition. Its aims were to provide an effective opposition to Labour, to avoid splitting the anti-Labour vote at elections, and eventually to oust the Labour government. Its political principles of freedom and free enterprise, though genuinely adhered to, were flexible of interpretation and readily subsumed under the more pressing negative aim of getting Labour out or keeping them out. Compared with Labour there is less scope, both formally and informally, for officials of the extra-parliamentary party to attempt to influence the parliamentary party in such matters as the formulation of party policy and the general determination of party tactics. The extra-parliamentary party is formally consulted to a certain extent, but the party conference acts more as a sounding-board for party members' views. In general, party activists in the extra-parliamentary party have been prepared to concentrate on organizing for elections and to leave policy matters to the parliamentary party.

61

The MPs, after all, are the section of the party most attuned to the strengths and weaknesses of the common enemy, Labour. For these reasons, National, for most of its history, has been able to concentrate more single-mindedly than Labour on the business of winning elections. The pursuit of power through electoral popularity has entailed little sense of compromise or betrayal, but has been legitimized by the valued mission of keeping New Zealand safe from Labour and socialism.

However, the difference between the two parties in this respect should not be exaggerated. One reason for the greater influence of the parliamentary members of the National party has been that between 1949 and 1984 they spent all but two three-year terms in office. MPs of either party are more likely to be deferred to when they are fortified by success at the polls and occupation of the Treasury benches. Constitutionally, as Labour has discovered in office, there may be more qualms about MPs receiving instructions from the extra-parliamentary party when they are ministers of the Crown than when they are merely members of a parliamentary opposition. Moreover, there have recently been some significant ideological changes both within and between the parties. In common with other western societies, New Zealand in the 1980s has seen the rise of right-wing liberalism, which has eclipsed socialism as the dominant intellectual movement in politics. The National Party, like right-wing parties elsewhere, has begun to experience the type of conflict between ideologues and pragmatists previously associated more with Labour parties. This began during the last term of the Muldoon government, particularly in reaction to the prime minister's increasingly interventionist approach to the economy, and has continued while the party has been in opposition. Some members enthusiastically endorse libertarian ethics and free market economics; others are more cautious, either because their economic interests are threatened by economic deregulation or because they favour a more conservative approach on moral and social issues or on defence. The ideological spectrum has been complicated by the Lange Labour government, which itself adopted the neo-liberal economic theory, thereby regaining Labour's traditional position as the programmatic party of ideas, even if the actual theory is in many respects the complete opposite of traditional socialist theory. National moderates have found themselves on some issues uneasily to the left not right of Labour. It remains to be seen whether Labour can sustain an economic policy which is against the interests and principles of many of its long-time supporters or whether National will desert its pragmatic past for a more doctrinaire future.

Though dogmatic adherence to unpopular party doctrine may

alienate the voters and make parties less democratically efficient, some doctrinal difference between the parties is essential. Parties, to remain effective, need some unifying principles or values other than the mere pursuit of their supporters' interests. The enthusiasm of the rank and file, so vital for maintaining the extra-parliamentary organization, may require the additional uplift which only the call to principle can provide. Unless there is some general consensus about what each party stands for, there will be little reason for different groups or interests to support one party rather than another. The long-term stability of the parties would then be weakened, as would their ability to attract and retain like-minded politicians who could form effective, cohesive governments. If both parties were to become entirely opportunistic in policy, the party system as we know it might break down and the voters might no longer be offered a choice between united and recognizably alternative party governments. Thus, some unifying principles, however flexible and ill-defined, are an important component of an effective party system.

The election policy

There are a number of ways in which the parties, through seeking electoral support, allow themselves to be influenced by the electorate. In the first place, each party offers an election policy or manifesto to the voters. For the winning party this becomes its mandate or the set of policies to which it is committed. The electoral mandate has been a vital part of democratic elections in New Zealand. It is especially important when there is a change of government and a party which has previously been in opposition becomes the government. On recent occasions when this has happened, in 1972, 1975 and 1984, the victorious opposition party has been elected with a very full and comprehensive party policy. In 1975, for instance, the National party issued about twenty separate policies covering all the main areas of government and electoral concern, such as agriculture, manufacturing, education, immigration, housing and so on. As in most election policies, many of the commitments were general in wording, promising to give 'more attention' or 'higher priority' to some problem. But there was also a considerable number of detailed and specific commitments. The policy on labour and industrial relations for instance, a thirteen-page document, contained general commitments to 'encourage profit sharing by workers and groups within industries' and to 'widen the use of the compulsory conference procedures'; it also included unambiguous commitments to increase the number of industrial mediators, to reinstate clauses defining illegal strikes which had been deleted from the

Industrial Relations Act by the Labour government and to include the freezing works as an essential industry under the first schedule of the Industrial Relations Act. Each of the separate policy statements together formed the official election policy to which all National candidates were bound. When the National party faced the electorate three years later in 1978, it followed the same course. It reissued an updated version of the 1975 policy, added a few more specific commitments but essentially stressed its claim to have lived up to the promises of the original policy, a claim which was backed up by the slogan 'we're keeping our word'. Labour, in the meantime, as the major party in opposition, prepared very detailed and comprehensive policies for the elections of 1978, 1981, and 1984, a pattern which has also been followed by the Democratic (formerly Social Credit) and New Zealand parties.

The authority of the election policy is far-reaching and widely recognized. It is clearly seen by members of the governing party as obliging them to act in certain ways. Specific promises will have to be kept; generally-worded intentions, if they do not require any definite course of action, will at least place limits on what policy options are politically possible. Governments know that, if they depart from their election policy, the political consequences in terms of unpopularity and damage to their credibility will be very great. Disappointed groups will be quick to howl their protests and the opposition will lose no opportunity of branding the government as immoral and unprincipled. Prime ministers, who carry such a large share of the responsibility for the popularity or unpopularity of their party, keep a particularly close watch on their government's performance in relation to the election policy.

During the 1972-5 Kirk Labour government, the prime minister's concern to adhere to the letter of the election policy seemed almost an obsession to departmental officials and ministers, who urged changes in prices and taxation levels to meet changing economic circumstances. The policy document earned the bitter nickname, 'the bloody red book'. Sir Robert Muldoon, when prime minister, also took his election policy statements very seriously. He kept a copy readily available in his room, and there was also another copy in the cabinet room which was regularly consulted at cabinet meetings. He was considerably embarrassed in 1977, on the vexed political question of sporting contacts with South Africa, when the party was shown to have committed itself to inconsistent positions. The official party policy, which became the government's policy, was that there would be no political interference in sport; this prevented the government from interfering to stop sporting contacts although leaving it free to express official disapproval of them. On the other hand, a shortened, glossier form of the election policy issued as a 'manifesto' had gone further and stated that the Springboks would be welcomed. The claim that the manifesto was written by an advertising agent and did not have the authority of the official party policy was greeted with considerable public criticism.

Similarly, the Lange Labour government was much criticized when it introduced a surtax on National Superannuation which was contrary to its electoral commitment to leave the structure of the superannuation scheme untouched. Moreover, the government's economic policy, so-called 'Rogernomics' (after the minister of finance, Mr Roger Douglas), was not foreshadowed in the 1984 party's election policy; indeed, it was not adopted until after the election. Because of the importance of this policy to the whole of the government's programme and to the following election campaign in 1987, the significance of the election policy was reduced. In 1987, Labour did not publish its full election policy statement until after the election. Mr Lange said during the campaign that manifestos did not matter and that governments should be judged on their actions. Some months after the 1987 election, the government introduced a state sector bill without consulting the state unions, a move which even the minister of state services admitted was in breach of the party's manifesto. Emboldened by its electoral victory and the endorsement of its economic strategy, the government was clearly prepared to continue to attack the power of sectional interests in the name of greater flexibility and efficiency, even if this meant breaking a clear commitment to a group from which it had drawn loyal support. In response to what they saw as cavalier treatment of electoral promises, the Labour party conference adopted a new rule allowing a 'manifesto vote', by which a two-thirds conference vote could force a policy into the party's manifesto. The deputy prime minister, however, said that a government could always refuse to carry out 'impracticable' policies. The Lange government had been careful to keep many of its specific 1984 promises: nuclear ships were banned from New Zealand ports; a ministry of women's affairs was established; the sixth form university entrance examination was abolished, and so on. None the less, its open disregard for election promises was a clear breach of political convention and, if it becomes politically acceptable, must mean a diminution in the people's trust in and power over their elected politicians.

The election policy serves as the set of principles which unify the governing caucus. Any attempt by an individual member of the parliamentary team to break with the party's programme can always be met with the objection that the member was elected as a party candidate committed to the declared programme. The more detailed the party's programme, the less room for open disagreement on policy among its members. The strict discipline characteristic of New Zealand parliamentary parties is thus linked to the fact that the parties' electoral programmes are full and specific. As the set of policies and general principles to which all are committed, the party programme is often used as the final arbiter of disputes within the party. Government backbenchers can use the election policy to bring ministers back into line. For instance, in recent National governments, on the issue of sporting contacts with South Africa, certain backbenchers were able to prevent moves by the government to express more than token opposition to Springbok tours by referring to the strong electoral commitment not to interfere. Conversely, the party leadership can use the election policy to restrain the initiative of backbenchers and keep them in line with government policy. The ground for dismissing the minister of works and development, Mr Derek Quigley, from the National cabinet in 1982 was that he had publicly endorsed opposition criticisms of the so-called 'growth strategy' which had been a prominent part of the government's platform in the election held only six months earlier.

Though fundamental to the democratic control of parliament, electoral mandates have no authority in law. This was demonstrated in 1975-6 when National came to power committed to abolishing Labour's superannuation scheme. Within weeks of the election, the prime minister announced that employers would no longer be required to make payments to the superannuation board; amendments to legislation would follow when parliament met later in the following year, but in the meantime employers would not be held liable for their contributions. Because the new government was clearly committed to abolishing the contributory scheme, temporary suspension of legislation was widely accepted, not only by grateful employers but also by such public officers as the chairman and members of the superannuation board and the auditor-general. However, the government was challenged in the courts and the chief justice held that its action was contrary to the Bill of Rights of 1688, which prevented the Crown from suspending laws without the consent of parliament. A constitutional crisis was avoided by allowing the government time in which to pass amending legislation. None the less, in law, the fact that the government was honouring an electoral commitment was irrelevant, another instance where constitutional law is out of step with political reality. Legally, the National government would have acted more properly if it had decided to let Labour's superannuation scheme continue indefinitely; in terms of political and constitutional convention, however, such defiance of a clear electoral commitment would have been much more shocking than the temporary suspension of legislation.

There is no doubt that the detailed party election policy places considerable limits on a government's freedom of action. All these limits are self-imposed by the party in order to gain or retain office, and are thus an instance of the people's power over the government. The parties put considerable time and effort into constructing their election policies. Some of the policies will be designed to have general appeal to voters as a whole, for instance, policies on inflation, health or any matter which affects the general consumer. Other policies will be aimed at particular sets of voters, for instance mortgage policies for first-home buyers, tax relief for parents of young children and so on. Still others will be designed for particular occupation groups, such as subsidies for farmers or higher bursaries for students, and may be worked out after close consultation with appropriate interest groups. Local or regional interests will be catered for by promises to aid local industry or expand public works. All such cases are instances of the power which these groups exercise over the government.

The power exercised by means of the election policy is indirect rather than direct. The parties limit their own actions in the hope of pleasing the voters; the voters at large do not take the initiative or issue direct demands to the parties. Unfortunately, the commitment which parties enter into is sometimes described in terms which suggest that they have received direct instructions from the people. The government may claim that it has been 'given a mandate' by the people or that in carrying out its electoral programme it is fulfilling 'the demands' of the electorate. Taken literally, such statements cannot be true. Only a certain section of the people will have voted for the winning party; moreover, most of the voters who did vote for the winning party will have been unaware of most of the specific policies listed in the election programme. Electoral research in New Zealand has tended to confirm findings in other Western democracies that the average voter is often unable to identify the policies which each party supports.

If the convention of the electoral mandate is understood to imply that the voters carefully weigh up all the detailed policies of each party before voting then it is obviously false. But this is not how the institution is seen to work either by the electors or by the politicians. The essence of the election mandate is not that the electorate literally instructs the elected government, but that each party, in soliciting support from the electorate, undertakes to enact certain policies if elected. The election policy is presented by the parties to the voters in an attempt to win votes. No one expects that all voters will be interested in all policies but only that some voters will be interested in each policy. The parties must make a commitment that every policy will be enacted, even if only a few voters will be aware of any of it. To break a commitment is to break faith with those voters who chose to vote for the party for that reason. Moreover, the breach of an electoral commitment will make the government appear generally untrustworthy and will jeopardize its support, even from those who did not know or care about the particular policy in question. Hence the very strong obligation on the party to enact all its election policy regardless of how many voters may or may not have been aware of each item in it. The strength of this obligation, together with the convention that requires parties to present the electorate with very detailed election policies, means that New Zealand governments are considerably constrained and limited in certain areas of public policy. In this way the voters exercise power over the politicians even if they, the voters, are ignorant of the policies and their actual voting decisions have not been influenced by these policies.

Responsiveness to the electorate

The election programme is but one of the ways in which the desire to win elections constrains the behaviour of governments. There is much that a government does which is not covered by its election policy, but which has some effect on its reputation with the voters and hence on its chances at the next election: how it manages the economy, how it reacts to the countless number of specific issues, national, sectional or local, which arise unpredictably and where the performance of the government is watched closely by the media and the public at large. In the mass of business which goes across a minister's desk the good politician will keep an eye open for anything with 'political' overtones that is likely to have repercussions for his party in the House or with the public at large. Such repercussions may ultimately have electoral consequences and the politician will make sure that these consequences are taken into account in making a decision. When a government's decision has been affected in this way by the politician's calculation of political advantages and disadvantages, we have another instance of the electorate's indirect power over the politician.

Such power is impossible to measure precisely. It is never easy to say how much an individual minister or cabinet as a whole has been guided in a particular decision by their political judgement of possible electoral consequences, and how much by their independent judgement of what is the best course of action regardless of political consequences. Discussions of political advantage often take place in secret and, if a government acts for reasons of electoral advantage, it may often try to cloak its motives under more respectable principles, such as the public interest or the good of some particular group. Though electoral ambition is one of the main instruments of the people's power over governments, there appears to be a general belief that this desire is somehow disreputable and not to be openly admitted — another instance of the conflict between some of our political values and the manner in which our political institutions actually function in a democratic manner. Another reason for the difficulty in tracing such influence is that politicians may not even be consciously aware of where political calculations take over from other motives. A good politician will be skilled at finding solutions which will not only please as many people as possible but will also be defensible on other grounds, such as long-term economic prosperity, consistency with previous policies and so on. Moreover, many apparently non-political reasons for action, such as the pursuit of long-term economic advantage, can become political, if such considerations seem to have an effect on the popularity of the government. None the less, in spite of the difficulty of separating out the precise effect of the electoral motive, we can still confidently say that much government policy is affected by it and would be decided very differently if the government did not have to face an election within three years or less.

All members of the ruling parliamentary party are involved in this electoral influence on government decision-making, because all stand to lose their jobs in the case of defeat. The prime minister has a particularly important part to play. Besides co-ordinating government business, he is also the manager of the party's electoral prospects. The appeal of the party leader has always been of critical importance to the electoral chances of a party, never more so than today when television is the main medium of political communication. A prime minister will owe his position to his colleagues' confidence that he is their best chance of winning and, in order to protect his own position, he will be under particular pressure to maintain or increase his rapport with the electorate. Also of importance in keeping a government on target for the next election are the backbenchers in the government caucus. Unlike ministers, they do not move their homes to Wellington but return to their homes in their constituencies at weekends. They are not caught up in the administrative details of departmental business or surrounded by departmental advisers. They are also more likely to represent marginal electorates, and thus to be more vulnerable to fluctuations in the government's popularity. For all these reasons, backbenchers are in particularly close touch with actual or likely public reactions to government policy. The weekly meetings of the government caucus are usually concerned with those items of government business which have a political or electoral significance, and ministers are most likely to take notice of backbench opinion when it is based on assessments of public opinion.

But how much notice is taken of backbench opinion? The number of ministers and under-secretaries is usually over twenty and, together with the whips, members of the executive usually have a majority in caucus. This is a high proportion in comparison with larger parliaments in other countries, and suggests that in New Zealand the cabinet is easily able to dominate caucus and that backbenchers are relatively powerless. Moreover, like any other similar group, caucus is likely to take its lead from its more senior and experienced members, almost all of whom will have found their way into the cabinet. Most backbenchers hope themselves to become ministers one day, and will be anxious to establish reputations for loyalty and reliability. Ministers also have the additional resources of information and advice provided by their departmental officers in the public service.

But, if ministers often seem to get their way in caucus, this does not mean that backbenchers exercise no indirect influence on them. Often cabinet will itself have anticipated the reaction of caucus. Because backbenchers do revolt from time to time and delay or modify particular government initiatives, the possibility of such resistance will influence the decisions ministers take and the recommendations they place before caucus. The intimacy of caucus, the frequent, familiar contact between ministers and backbenchers means that most influence exerted within caucus will be indirect, often even unconscious, and not susceptible of ready observation or clear-cut analysis. Though backbenchers may be more in touch with electorate opinion, cabinet ministers are themselves experienced politicians and often alive to possible electoral consequences. It would be a mistake to see ministers as always representing a non-political, departmental viewpoint or backbenchers as the sole source of popular influence within caucus. All members of caucus are electorally sensitive and all will make some contribution to keeping the party in tune with the electorate. From this point of view it is perhaps less significant that ministers may be able to dominate backbenchers, than that such a high proportion of caucus is able to hold office in the government.

If politicians are to be concerned about the electoral consequences of their actions they must assume that their actions can have electoral consequences, that the way people vote is determined, at least in part, by their opinions of how the governing party has performed and how it compares with the likely performance of the opposition. This assumption, that the voters act 'rationally', choosing the party that they think will give them most of what they want or least of what they do not want, has been challenged by research into voting behaviour. Surveys aimed at discovering why people vote the way they do have suggested that apparently 'non-rational' factors, such as family loyalties, social background or unthinking habit, are the most likely. If this conclusion were correct, politicians would themselves be acting irrationally if they expected voters to decide which way to vote on the the basis of the parties' performance.

However, such extreme scepticism about the motives of voters is not warranted. Certainly, the notion of the completely rational voter is unrealistic. There are few, if any, voters who scrutinize each party's programme in detail, and whose choice is determined solely by a careful calculation of which party will benefit them most, without any influence of previous loyalties or affections. On the other hand, few voters are entirely irrational, completely uninfluenced by any view, however general, of how the different parties have governed or are likely to govern. Political preferences may be formed first within the family and the social milieu of parents, but they are later tested against the actual interests of the adult voter. That people tend to remain loyal to one party or to vote the same way as their parents and friends does not convict them of being unthinking voters. After all, most people's interests remain fairly constant and similar to those of their family and friends. Traditional party loyalties, for instance those of farmers who always vote National or trade unionists who always vote Labour, are not without material foundations; they are continually reinforced by benefits given or promised by the respective parties to their supporters. For instance, a National party which consistently acted less as the farmer's friend and more as the unionist's friend, could not count on maintaining its traditional support for long. People's perception of the parties may be imprecise, their knowledge of detailed manifestos negligible, but their decision to vote is in most cases at least informed by a general impression of the relative performance, actual and potential, of the contending parties. How this impression is formed, how it is affected by particular party actions or decisions, remains complex and obscure. Fortunately for democrats, however, politicians cannot afford the luxury of too much scepticism. Only a

71

small number of votes may make the difference between winning and losing an election. All that is needed to provoke the politician into responding to the electorate is the likelihood that some voters, not necessarily all, may react to a particular decision or policy, a possibility that it will often be foolhardy to overlook.

The degree of likely electoral reaction varies with the type of issue. Some issues, such as whether to introduce a new form of taxation or whether to impose charges for medical prescriptions, are highly political in nature. They are bound to receive a lot of media attention and the opposition will be alert to any opportunity to mobilize public discontent. The decisions will be taken in a highly political atmosphere, and it is likely that caucus committees and caucus as a whole will be closely involved. Other issues may have negligible political overtones. The minister of health, for instance, may be required to approve new conditions of work for hospital registrars. Interested parties in the medical profession and the hospital service may be consulted, but there will be no need to refer the matter to caucus or to consider potential votes won or lost according to the decision. On all government business, it is true, there is a general incentive for ministers to manage public affairs competently and honestly: every ministerial decision is potentially embarrassing to the party, if some culpable administrative mistake is discovered. The relationship between the minister of lands and the marginal lands board, for instance, would normally be quite uncontentious but in 1980, after charges of undue ministerial influence and nepotism, it became a highly publicized issue which may have hurt the National party electorally. Administration within the department of Maori affairs, usually routine, in 1986 suddenly escalated into the 'Maori loans affair' which permanently discredited the minister and seriously embarrassed the Labour government.

Publicity, particularly publicity of actions which may embarrass the governing party, is essential to the democratic responsiveness of government. Unless members of the government fear that potentially unpopular measures will become widely known, they will have little incentive to refrain from taking them. In general, by world standards New Zealand can claim to have an open system of government. The proceedings of parliament, where all legislation and expenditure must be approved and where ministers must answer for the conduct of their portfolios, are open to the public and to the media. The press and broadcasting are legally free within the limits of the laws of indecency and defamation. Yet much of the day-to-day work of government is still carried on in secret. The collective responsibility of cabinet requires the government to appear united, and means that any discussion and disagreement must be kept confidential to the cabinet or committee room. Similarly, the detailed information and advice which public servants give to ministers is also confidential, although the Official Information Act (1982) has helped to open more departmental documents up to public view and criticism.

The opposition's ability to probe and publicize the weak points of government is weakened by the individual MP's heavy workload and the superior resources at the disposal of the governing party. Coverage of politics in broadcasting and the press is hampered by the small scale of the New Zealand media. Hard-pressed journalists rush from one press briefing to another, with little time to investigate on their own initiative. Political reporting, however, is largely free of bias, although, editorially, the press tends to be conservative and opposed to trade unions while current affairs programmes on television have often conveyed an image of the smart left-of-centre or 'trendy left'. More dangerous is the way in which politicians can intimidate the media. A number of factors, such as the intimacy of New Zealand political life, the close relations between politicians, journalists and editors, broadcasting's dependence on government for empowering legislation and finance, as well as the strictness of the rules of parliamentary privilege and the law of defamation, all help to impede the critical independence of the media necessary to make governments democratically responsive to the public.

Another factor which may affect the extent of electoral influence is timing. The closer the next election, the more anxious a government will be to increase its support from the electorate and avoid offending any important section of voters. Governments do not like to take hard and unpalatable decisions in election years. They try to confine their unpopular measures to the early part of their term of office, in the hope that such measures will have been forgotten or will have yielded more popular results before the next election. The belief that issues relatively distant in time have less electoral effect than more immediate issues is plausible but difficult to prove conclusively. There are obvious exceptions. For instance, Labour's so-called 'Black Budget' in 1958 and the cancellation of the Springbok tour in 1973 both occurred more than two years before the next election, but both became lively and apparently influential election issues. At the most, proximity to an election may be one factor but not an overriding one in determining which issues are electorally significant. If governments try particularly hard not to be unpopular in election years, the people generally exercise more power and there is, therefore, more democracy in election years than in other years of a government's term of office. For the same reason, it follows that the shorter period of time between elections, the more democratic the political system is likely to be. New Zealand, with its three-year parliamentary term is, in this respect, among the more democratic of modern parliamentary democracies. None stipulates a shorter term and most have a longer term of four or five years. Comparisons are complicated because New Zealand governments have made relatively little use of their discretion to call an election before the end of their term. Governments appear reluctant to call an early election, unless in a grave national or political crisis, because to do so would be seen as an unjustified attempt to exploit a short-term advantage and would be likely to rebound upon the governing party. This view was confirmed by National's defeat in 1984 when the election was called four months earlier than necessary for an unconvincing reason (the prime minister claimed, implausibly, that he could not count on majority support in the House). Before that, the last snap election was more than thirty years earlier, in the aftermath of the 1951 waterfront strike.

The democratic power of elections is arguably greater in a political system where early elections are normal practice and where, therefore, every year is potentially an election year and government is carried on in a highly political atmosphere. On the other hand, such an established practice does place undue initiative in the hands of the government, giving it the sole power to call a snap election and, conversely, giving it the right to sit out its full term if its chances of winning earlier appear remote. A relatively short, fixed term between elections is thus the only means of guaranteeing that governments will remain reasonably vulnerable to electoral unpopularity. New Zealanders' preference for the three-year term was confirmed in 1967 when the question of extending the term of parliament to four years was put to a referendum and resoundingly defeated. The term of parliament was one of the issues covered by the Royal Commission on the Electoral System, which was set up by the Lange Labour government and reported in 1986. The Commission saw some possible advantages in a longer, four-year term, which would give a government more time to implement policies and the voters more time to judge their effects. On the other hand, it recognized the need for voters to be able to call elected governments to account and was not in favour of extending the term of parliament unless alternative means were introduced of checking the potentially undemocratic actions of governments.

Ministers and the public service

If the governing party is to be an instrument of popular power, it must be not only sensitive to the likely reactions of the electorate but also capable of translating its preferences into concrete government action; that is, it must be able to exercise political control over the bureaucracy, the public service. How effective is this political control? There is little doubt about the official, legal position: the highest authority is given to statutes which the governing party has the power to enact or amend through its control of parliament; next in importance come cabinet minutes, the formal resolutions passed at cabinet meetings; within particular departments, ministerial directives take precedence over any decision by departmental officers. Permanent officials clearly recognize the duty of an elected government to enact its mandate. On a change of government, departments will prepare draft policies for the incoming ministers based on the various commitments in their election policy. However, ministers cannot determine every action that a department takes. The sheer size of the public service makes this impossible. The forty departments of the public service employ over 80,000 people (excluding those state servants in the police, teaching and hospital services). Cabinet ministers can therefore have direct control over only a minute fraction of the business conducted by their departments.

Indirect control and anticipated reactions spread their influence more widely. Senior officials have to be politically sensitive, aware of what types of recommendation will fit the government's general aims and ready to enhance their ministers' political standing in the government and with the public generally. In this respect, they are their ministers' political as well as their administrative agents. Such political support for the government of the day is not confined to the those few senior officials who have regular personal dealings with ministers. A survey of middle-ranking public servants showed that they were very conscious of the political environment, and accepted a clear responsibility to help formulate government policy and to administer it faithfully. The tradition of political neutrality thus does not prevent public servants from performing actions which may have partisan political overtones; it merely requires them to serve whichever party is in power with equal conscientiousness.

On the other hand, public servants often resent what they see as undue political influence in public administration, particularly when ministers make adjustments for blatant reasons of electoral popularity or to appease pressure from interested parties. Moreover, many departments have their own independent and firmly held policy preferences which they will attempt to persuade a minister to adopt. Where the minister's plans are contrary to the department's, the officials may try to deflect his or her purpose, pointing out practical and administrative difficulties, and doing little to prevent Treasury, which holds the purse strings, from defeating their minister's proposals. Under the Lange government, Treasury itself has emerged as a highly influential independent source of policy initiatives. Much clearly depends on the individual minister's personality and ability. Some ministers can impose their wishes and those of their party on a department; others let their officials run them and may find themselves supporting policies which are unpopular with their cabinet and caucus colleagues and likely to damage their party's standing with the electorate. Against a determined minister, public servants will certainly accept temporary defeat. But, in the revealing words of one permanent head, the department 'lives to fight another day'. If immediate authority rests with the minister of the day, time is often on the side of the permanent officials.

The difficulties of extending political influence over the public service are increased by the traditions of secrecy and confidentiality surrounding the conduct of government business. The doctrine of ministerial responsibility has required that only ministers should speak for their departments and has discouraged public servants from speaking openly about departmental policies and the reasons behind them. Paradoxically, however, while the doctrine is intended to protect the authority of ministers, the less publicity an issue has, the harder it may be for ministers to impose their will on public servants. When public interest and controversy have been aroused, the politician can more plausibly claim to be acting on behalf of public opinion or anticipating a likely reaction from the electorate. Conversely, when the topic is one which few know about, the weight of departmental numbers and experience is likely to prevail. In recent years, however, departmental reports and working papers have become more widely available as a result of the Official Information Act and government initiatives, such as 'opening the books' after the 1984 election. It has become easier to know, for instance, the 'Treasury view' or the 'Department of Education view' on certain policy issues. This broadening of public debate should enable politicians to act on behalf of a better informed public opinion. At the same time, it reflects an evolution in conventions of ministerial responsibility. Greater publicity for departmental views opens a public gap between politicians and officials. Ministers are less constrained from publicly criticizing public servants. In 1984, the minister of works in the National government, Mr Friedlander, publicly attacked officers of his own department, the Ministry of Works, for negligence connected with cost overruns for irrigation schemes in central Otago. There is now a converse danger that exposure to political criticism may undermine the public servants' loyalty to the government of the day.

Political control of the public service also depends on the effectiveness of parliamentary scrutiny of legislation and public administration. Much of this work is done through the system of parliamentary select committees, which examine proposed legislation and interview public servants and other interested parties. The scope and activities of parliamentary committees have increased steadily over the last twenty years. At present there are thirteen subject committees, each with five members and each covering a major area of government, such as finance and expenditure, education and science, foreign affairs and defence. Besides scrutinizing proposed legislation, all select committees now also have the power to initiate their own inquiries into areas of government administration. However, although the work of the committees is certainly of growing importance, the small number of backbench MPs in a House of fewer than 100 members, the need to give first priority to proposed legislation together with the pressure on MPs' time from constituency and other work, mean that the committees can only scratch the surface of public administration. Moreover, in a system of parliamentary party government, where the main function of MPs is to defend or attack the government, a non-partisan approach to committee work is difficult to sustain. Much useful work can be, and is, done by committees when they operate quietly, outside the reach of publicity or political controversy. However, once the issue becomes one which affects the political fortunes of either party, MPs can no longer afford not to be partisan. It is a mistake to expect the degree of independence and public leverage which congressional committees display in the United States. Because of the constitutional separation of powers, the United States executive does not depend on a majority in the legislature and individual members of congress can afford to act more independently.

The claim is often made, particularly by backbench and opposition MPs, that the executive has gained too much power at the expense of parliament. Stated generally and without qualification, this may mislead if it suggests that the right of the governing party to control the agenda and decisions of parliament is illegitimate; in this sense 'executive' domination of parliament is an essential feature of parliamentary democracy. On the other hand, it is undoubtedly true that the permanent part of the executive, that is the public service, is not adequately supervised by its political masters in parliament. Though the influence of the governing caucus and its ministers may run some way into the affairs of government departments, the bulk of departmental business is largely unaffected. Lack of such political control does not necessarily imply a complete absence of democratic accountability. Many decisions will be subject to other types of democratic influence, particularly pressure from the interest group system, to be discussed in the next chapter. Other decisions may be better freed altogether from political control. This is one of the reasons behind the establishment of state owned enterprises to take over the trading functions formerly performed by government departments such as the Post Office and the Department of Energy. If a service is to be provided to the consumer, the best means of democratic accountability, it is argued, is through the decisions of individual consumers conveyed directly by the market rather than through electoral influence relayed indirectly and ineffectively by politicians. Whether the various mechanisms of public control, through the various systems specified in the model, actually provide the people with sufficient democratic control of government policy is a question which will be taken up in the final chapter. There are, however, serious limits to the ability of parliamentary parties to exercise control over the permanent bureaucracy.

Equality among voters?

Elections operate as mechanisms of democratic power, encouraging politicians to make political decisions which will maintain or increase the chances of the party at the next election. But democracy involves not just the exercise of power by the people but also the equal exercise of such power. To what extent do the actual conduct of elections and the rules which govern their operation allow each member of the electorate to exercise an equal degree of power over politicians? Do the political parties, in their pursuit of electoral success, appeal equally to all groups and interests, or do some people exercise more than their fair share of power and others less? Does the electoral system itself count each person's vote equally or are some voters penalized by the way in which constituency boundaries are drawn, or by the method of translating votes for parties into seats in parliament?

In the first place, do the parties appeal to all groups? Each of the major parties draws particular support from particular groups in the community. The National party has always received strong support from farmers and those associated with the farming industry. It also polls well among the more well-to-do business and professional classes in both town and country. Labour has drawn its votes most heavily from the less well-off, unskilled and manual workers and trade unionists, but it also has important areas of middle-class and white-collar support. Neither party can take its traditional support for granted. Die-hard supporters of Labour or National may be unlikely to vote for the other major party, but they can, if disgruntled, damage their party's chances by abstaining from voting or by registering a 'protest' vote for a third party, such as the Democratic or New Zealand party; disaffection among party stalwarts will be quickly reflected by party activists in the extra-parliamentary party whose support is vital for success at the polls. Parliamentary parties must take care to give more attention than their opponents to the interests of their traditional supporters, and to pay more than lip-service to the political principles which support these interests.

At the same time, neither party can afford to ignore the wishes of other major sections of the electorate, even those groups from which it is least likely to win much support. Part of the reason lies in the pressure all governments face from interest groups representing most major sections of the country. As we shall see in the next chapter, the interest group system can provide a degree of countervailing power to balance the more partisan tendencies of political parties. Another related factor is the effect of general political conventions and values. In New Zealand, as in most reasonably open societies, governments are expected to justify and defend their actions in terms of such concepts as the public good or the national interest. Such terms are imprecise in application and can be used to cloak the special interests of a section of the community. But they do set limits on possible action that governments can take. For instance, a National government wishing to guarantee high incomes to farmers must be prepared to face the objection that subsidies discourage developments in more productive land use, or are unfair in relation to the burden being carried by other taxpayers. In answering such criticisms in parliament and the media government spokesmen cannot simply reply that the farmers are their friends whom they want to look after. Such blatant partisanship could cause adverse public reaction and be politically damaging. The need to offer a reasoned defence in terms of equity or the national interest, though it may still leave room for some partiality towards farmers, still places some limits on unscrupulous favouritism.

A further factor discouraging excessive polarization between the parties is the complex nature of the 'floating' vote, that is the votes of those who are not committed to either party and who, in effect, determine the outcome of elections. Floating voters are of many different types: they may oscillate between one party and another; they may support only one party, but intermittently float in and out of voting and abstention; they may be first-time voters, as yet with no fixed political preferences. They are found in all sections of society. Though there are social groups which are predominantly Labour or predominantly National, there are always some in each group who vote against their social norm, either consistently, or from time to time as floating voters. The factors influencing voting behaviour are many and complex. Social class or occupational interest may be the most important single factor but there are many others such as parental influence, local political traditions, religious or ideological conviction, which may produce countervailing pressures. Because support for a party may come from members of any social group, parties are under pressure to appeal, at least to some extent, to all sections of the community. If the voting map were not so blurred, and parties could hope to win virtually the whole of certain sections of the community, they could more easily ignore the rest. After all, a party needs to win only a majority of seats in parliament for which not even a majority of votes is necessary. The result would be governments which favoured certain sections of the community much more markedly and other groups not at all. But this is not the case. National and Labour governments may differ in emphasis from one another, but neither can afford altogether to alienate any major section of the community.

New Zealanders have always been relatively assiduous in exercising their right to vote. Of those registered to vote by being on the electoral roll, about 90 per cent actually vote (in 1984, 94 per cent; in 1987, 89 per cent). Registration, although compulsory, is not legally enforced, and comparison with the more accurate census figures suggests that about 5 per cent of eligible voters remain unregistered, thus reducing the turn-out percentage of eligible voters to around 85 per cent. This percentage is high by world standards.

Are non-voters a cross-section of New Zealand society or are particular social groups disproportionately found among their number? Research has suggested that young, newly qualified voters, single women and members of lower socio-economic groups, are slightly less likely to vote than the rest of the population. Maori and Pacific Islanders tend to vote less than Pakeha members of the population in local elections and the same trend probably occurs at the national level. What effect has this had in terms of responsiveness of the politicians to the electorate?

In particular, do those groups who are less likely to vote receive correspondingly less attention from the political parties? No firm evidence is available. Sometimes an under-participating group may become the object of special attention as a potential area of relatively untapped support. In 1981, for instance, all parties, some rather belatedly, introduced policies specifically aimed at the youth vote which appeared likely to be crucial in deciding the result. Polynesians, both Maori and Islanders, fare less well in New Zealand society; they are more likely than other New Zealanders to be unemployed or in low-paid and unskilled work, ill-housed or under-nourished. But it is not clear how far this is due to any alienation from the electoral system and how far it is the result of other political and social factors. In the case of Maori, there is the additional question, to be discussed below, of whether the separate Maori roll adversely affects their electoral influence. As we shall see when we examine the power of interest groups, some groups are clearly much more effective than others in exercising influence over government. But in so far as political power is exercised through political parties competing for victory at elections, it is much more equally distributed. In the ballot box each person's vote counts equally with everyone else's. Variations in turnout for different groups must be set against a background of consistently high overall turnout, which means that each person is seen by the political parties as a potential voter whose vote may make a difference to the outcome.

Electoral equality: Maori representation

But is it true that each person's vote has an equal chance of determining the outcome? Is not the electoral system itself biased in favour of certain areas of the population? This raises the question of how the electoral system in New Zealand translates the sum total of individual votes into seats in parliament, and whether each person's vote is equally effective in the process. One important aspect of the electoral system is the element of separate ethnic representation through the Maori seats in parliament. These four seats were introduced in the nineteenth century as a way of guaranteeing parliamentary representation to the Maori as landowners and British subjects, and at the same time preventing them from swamping the votes of the settlers in the remaining seats which were reserved for Europeans. Whatever the cynicism surrounding their origins, the Maori seats helped Maori to participate in what was an alien system of government, and have ensured that Maori interests and the Maori people are visibly represented in parliament. In an electoral system consisting of single member constituencies, it is not easy for members of an ethnic minority to elect their own representatives to parliament unless they are heavily concentrated in certain territorial areas. Although Maori MPs have been elected for general electorates, particularly in the National party, many Maori people argue that such MPs cannot adequately represent specifically Maori interests and values if they must also retain the support of their Pakeha constituents.

It might be thought that the practice of separate ethnic representation is inherently undemocratic. In terms of democratic principle, however, the only requirement is that each vote should count equally. The fact that constituencies have usually been made out of unified territorial areas is mainly a matter of historical tradition and convenience. Localities have common interests which their MPs can represent; local constituencies facilitate contact between the representative and the represented. But other criteria, based on other similarities of interest, are, in principle at least, compatible with democracy. For instance, constituencies could be drawn up on the basis of occupational groups, with MPs for sheep farmers, school teachers, pensioners, and so on. Feminists might wish to see gender as a criterion, thus ensuring that half the MPs were elected solely by women. Again, age could be the criterion with MPs selected to represent different age-groups. These criteria might be impractical, but they would not be undemocratic, provided that the number of representatives for each group was equal in proportion to the size of the group. In terms of democratic principle, the same should apply to electorates based on race, particularly in a multi-cultural society, where ethnic minorities are not concentrated in particular geographical regions and are therefore not guaranteed representation through conventional territorial constituencies.

Ethnic representation, however, though democratically acceptable if fairly administered, does present peculiar difficulties, both moral and practical. The whole notion of making any political distinctions based on race has, for some people, been morally discredited because such distinctions have most commonly been used as a basis for systematic exploitation of one racial group by another. There are many New Zealanders who consider that, in the interests of racial harmony, the question of what race anyone belongs to is not a question which should be publicly asked at all. Moreover, given the amount of intermarriage between Pakeha and Maori, it is not easy to determine who is and who is not a Maori. Authorities are properly reluctant to investigate the sensitive and complex question of a citizen's racial background. The question of Maori identification has therefore been left up to each individual and has become a matter more of cultural affirmation than racial ancestry. In general, these difficulties and misgivings, together with Pakeha guilt about the sins of the past, add up to a sense of public embarrassment about the Maori seats. Historically, they may have been justifiable in terms of a constitutional commitment to recognize the rights of an indigenous people. None the less, the doubts about whether they are morally defensible and consistent with democratic principles may help to explain why they remained for so long an unsatisfactory administrative mess.

For many years, elections to the Maori seats were treated very differently from the main election. Voting was held on a different day until 1951 and the secret ballot, first introduced for European electorates in 1870, was not extended to the Maori electorates until 1937. In contrast to the regular adjustments to the boundaries of the European electorates, the boundaries of the Maori seats remained unchanged for decades at a time. The rules governing the Maori seats were not included in the entrenched sections of the Electoral Act, that is those sections which can be amended only by a three-quarters majority of the house or by a referendum. Thus, the Maori seats are not, as the principles of electoral law should be, clearly elevated above the party struggle. These administrative differences may have been due to an unreflective double standard rather than to deliberate prejudice, but they did give rise to charges of second-class treatment for Maori voters.

In recent years, considerable improvements have been made in the administration of the Maori seats. Until 1975, those of more than half Maori descent were required to register on the Maori roll, those with less than half on the 'European' roll, with half-castes being allowed to choose. Since then, reference to the fractions of descent has been removed in line with the new emphasis on self-identification rather than the degree of descent as the main criterion of Maori identity, and all Maori voters have been given the choice of enrolling on either the Maori or the 'general' roll (as it is now called). A nationwide 'Maori option' is held after each five-yearly census as a prelude to the five-yearly adjustment of electoral boundaries. In 1981, the representation commission was given authority to make five-yearly adjustments to the boundaries of the four seats, taking into account movement of the Maori population and tribal boundaries. The definition of the Maori poulation now used by the commission includes not only those on the Maori roll, but also an estimate of their children. This means that the children of Maori voters are no longer counted in the electoral population used for calculating the number of general electorates and their boundaries. This removed the source of the grievance, felt by many Maori voters, that their children were being used to increase the number of non-Maori MPs. The particular difficulties which Maori voters face when voting have also been reduced. Because only a certain fraction of polling booths are designated as Maori polling booths, Maori voters attempting to vote at a polling booth not so designated, even if it is within their electorate and the closest booth to where they live, have had to cast a 'special' vote, like general voters who vote outside their own electorate. This is a more complicated process than normal voting and more likely to lead to invalid voting. At the 1987 election, a much simplified form of special vote, the 'Tangata Whenua' vote, was introduced for Maori voters.

However, a number of more intractable difficulties still remain. One is that Maori voters are not allowed to change to or from the Maori roll at times other than at the five-yearly option. This is to preserve the equity of the electoral redistribution based on the five-yearly figures and to prevent Maori voters from changing rolls for tactical purposes after the boundaries have been announced. None the less, individual political attitudes and preferences may genuinely develop and change significantly over a period of five years, and the embargo is felt by many to be an unjustified and inequitable restriction of their voting rights. Another disadvantage arises from the fact that Maori adults are much more likely than Pakeha adults to be unregistered on either roll. Only one in ten of those of voting age is of Maori descent and eligible to enrol on the Maori roll. However, of those eligible voters who are unregistered (about 5 per cent of the eligible population), a much higher fraction, perhaps as many as one in three, are of Maori descent. The representation commission includes all these unregistered potential Maori voters in the total electoral population. They therefore help to increase the number of general electorates by one or two seats.

This may not seem a significant factor, but it is particularly wounding to Maori people when compared with the fact that the number of Maori seats is held static at four, regardless of how many voters enrol on the Maori roll. Given the great concern for electoral equality in the rest of the electoral system, the fixed number of Maori seats is a glaring undemocratic anomaly. Some have argued that the number of seats should be decided in relation to the number who declare themselves to be Maori in the census, regardless of whether they eventually register on the Maori or the general roll. This would certainly increase the number of seats but would, in turn, be contrary to the principle of one vote, one value. If Maori voters are to continue to have the option of voting in either general or Maori electorates, the only democratically satisfactory solution is to make the number of Maori and general seats proportionate to the size of the Maori and general rolls. If this were done on the basis of the present Maori roll, the number of Maori seats, it has been estimated, would be the same as at present, that is four.

The principle, however, would be different and, once the exercise of the Maori option was known to affect the number of Maori seats, the size of the Maori roll could increase. There would be pressure on Maori voters to choose the Maori rather than the general roll and so maintain and possibly increase the number of Maori seats. At present, a considerable number of self-identifying Maori opt for the general roll because, for example, they are strong Labour or National supporters and want to vote where their vote may make a difference to the final result of the election and not 'waste' their vote in one of the Maori electorates which are invariably safe for Labour. They can opt for the general roll without directly threatening the survival of the four Maori seats. However, if the number of seats were to vary with the number opting for the Maori roll, the situation would be changed. Maori who opted for the general roll would be affecting the number of seats and would be made to feel traitors to their race. Indeed, a major consequence of allowing the number of seats to vary would be to introduce an element of political competition and potential racial conflict into the registration process. The five-yearly option could become a bitter campaign, conducted on racially divided lines, between the supporters and opponents of separate Maori representation. Democratic justice between the races would come at a high price in terms of increased racial tension and hostility. The dilemma of either continuing with a static number of seats, which is inequitable, or of varying the number, which is racially inflammatory, provides a powerful argument for an alternative electoral system which would guarantee Maori representation without the divisiveness of a separate Maori roll.

Another disadvantage of the present method of separate representation for Maori voters is that it has reduced the degree of political leverage which Maori voters deserve in terms of their numbers. Since the 1930s, the Maori seats have all been safe for Labour. Though Maori voters have wavered in the degree of support for Labour, either by abstaining or by voting for another party, none of the Maori seats has been lost by Labour. The independent Maori party, Mana Motuhake, was unable to win a seat even in the most favourable circumstances, at the Northern Maori by-election in 1980 when its leader, the well-known former Labour minister Matiu Rata, was its candidate. The National party has never come close to winning any of the seats. Thus neither of the major parties has much electoral incentive to pay attention to the wishes of Maori voters. At the same time, MPs in the general seats can afford to ignore Maori interests as not being their concern but the preserve of the Maori MPs. They are thus deprived of the degree of regular contact with Maori communities in their areas which they would be forced into if they were their official representatives. Maori voters can sometimes get good individual service from their MPs who work hard to cover very large constituencies (Southern Maori covers the area of forty-five general electorates). However, the fact that they do not have direct links with the general MPs in their localities helps to keep them and their interests out of the mainstream of New Zealand politics. In this respect, it can be argued, the Maori seats operate as a political ghetto, guaranteeing separate, formal representation, but denying real influence. However, abolition of a separate Maori roll and separate Maori seats under the present electoral system would almost certainly prevent the election of Maori MPs who would be recognized by Maori groups as genuinely representative of Maori interests.

One of the great advantages of the mixed member proportional system proposed by the Royal Commission on the Electoral System is that it would provide a way out of these difficulties. Under this system, half the members are elected from single-member constituencies and half from party lists drawn up by political parties. Maori voters would vote for their local constituency members on a common electoral roll. Political parties could be expected (they could even be legally required) to include Maori candidates high on their party lists. These candidates would be selected by the Maori sections within each party. They would not be required to appeal to all sections of the electorate, but could concentrate on specifically Maori issues as do the present Maori MPs. Thus Maori voters could become better integrated into national political processes while still having specifically Maori MPs, a combination which is not possible under the present electoral system.

Electoral equality: votes and seats

Apart from the issue of Maori representation, how fair and equal is the New Zealand electoral system to the individual voter? One obvious way in which the voters may or may not be treated equally is in the drawing up of constituencies. If some constituencies contain significantly fewer voters than others, the individual voters in smaller constituencies will have disproportionate power because their votes will make a more significant contribution to the final outcome. With the partial exception of the Maori seats, New Zealand electoral law places a very high value on the equality of numbers in electorates. Constituency boundaries are redrawn after each five-yearly census by an independent representation commission. In redrawing boundaries, very close attention is paid to achieving maximum equality. As twenty-five seats are allocated to the South Island, the quota or norm for each electorate is obtained by calculating one twenty-fifth of the South Island's 'electoral population', which is the total population, children as well as adults, less those on the Maori roll and an estimate of their children. The North Island seats are then allocated in proportion. In drawing boundaries the commission is allowed to deviate no more than 5 per cent from the quota, a low degree of 'tolerance' in comparison with other electoral systems. However, the numbers of voters who actually enrol for each constituency vary more widely; at this final stage the maximum variation is closer to 20 per cent rather than 5 per cent. One reason is that the representation commission uses total rather than adult population and the proportion of the population under the voting age varies considerably between constituencies. In this respect, it is not so much adult voters who are being equally represented as the whole population, children as well as adults. Other variations in the numbers actually enrolled are due to shifts of population after the census is taken and to differences in the numbers of unregistered voters.

The quest for numerical equality carries a certain price. Constituencies are often highly artificial segments of territory, cutting across well-established geographical or local body boundaries. Local interests may thus be less effectively represented in parliament than they would be if a greater tolerance allowed constituency boundaries to follow local communities of interest more closely. On the other hand, the variegated nature of many constituencies may help to keep MPs concerned about matters of interest to more than one section of the community. More damaging is the dislocation caused by the frequency of redistribution, particularly in the North Island. Every five years some constituencies are drastically redrawn, others disappear altogether and new ones are created. The disruption to the careers of MPs and to their relations with constituents as well as to the political parties in general is considerable. It may actually weaken the sensitivity of parliament to the individual citizen which redistribution is designed to enhance.

At one time, extra weight was deliberately given to the votes of the rural population. From the 1880s until after the Second World War when it was finally abolished by the Labour government, the so-called 'country quota' ensured that rural electorates were artificially inflated by adding 28 per cent to their actual population. The effect was to add up to about eight extra seats to the rural areas. The justification, apart from the natural advantage to those politicians and parties who represented rural interests, was that in the country the population was more widely scattered and transport was more time-consuming, making contact between representative and constituents especially difficult. In addition, farming was the major export industry and the basis of the nation's wealth; the rural interest, it could be argued, deserved to exercise disproportionate influence on the government. Few would now support these arguments, at least as justifications of a weighting in favour of the rural voter. Transport and communications have greatly improved, though rural MPs must still face a disproportionate amount of time spent in travelling in their electorates. The importance of the farming industry is not as overwhelming as fifty years ago. At any rate, farmers are able to exercise at least their fair share of political influence through normal parliamentary and interest group channels, without needing the additional help of special weighting in the electoral system. There is still, however, a residual element of country quota in the electoral distribution: rural electorates tend to be nearer the minimum than the maximum population allowed for each electorate. Moreover, as the proportion of children in the population was traditionally higher in the country than in towns, rural areas benefited from the calculation of constituency size by total population, that is eligible voters together with those under voting age. In recent years, however, this advantage has diminished as the rural birth-rate has declined and some urban constituencies now have a particularly high ratio of children.

Though each vote carries roughly equal weight within each constituency, the number of seats in parliament won by each party is far from equal to its share of votes. This is a consequence of the single-member plurality type of electoral system that New Zealand inherited from Britain. Originally this system was mainly intended to select a local representative who would speak on behalf of the local community in a national assembly. This function still persists, but, since the development of nationwide political parties, the main focus of elections has become national rather than local and the main choice is not of individual local representatives but of a party government. The demands of equity and fairness have shifted accordingly. It is no longer sufficient simply to have equality in the choice of a local MP; one must also have an equal say in the choice of which party or parties should govern. A single-member plurality system, such as New Zealand's, clearly distorts the proportions between numbers of votes cast and parliamentary seats won. The major parties regularly win a higher percentage of seats than they do of votes. The governing party typically has a majority of seats without a majority of votes. At the same time, minor parties, such as the Democratic (formerly Social Credit) party or the New Zealand party have attracted a significant share of the votes while winning few or no seats. Such discrepancies naturally give rise to complaints that the electoral system is unfair. There is increasing support for electoral reform, to bring representation in parliament more into line with the national distribution of support for the different parties.

A comprehensive study of the complex subject of proportional representation and the varieties of alternative electoral procedures is beyond the scope of this book. The issues have recently been extensively covered, from a New Zealand perspective, in the report of the Royal Commission on the Electoral System which recommended a mixed member proportional system based on the West German system. Some general comments, however, may be made from the point of view of the model of democratic government we have adopted. The model stresses the function of elections as a choice between alternative party governments, each bidding for a majority of votes. It also sees democratic virtue in the ability of a government to control parliament. If the government can rely on a cohesive parliamentary majority, it is much more likely to be able to govern effectively when enacting its mandate and responding to pressure from the electorate. From this point of view, the bias in favour of larger parties may be considered a source of strength: it simplifies the voters' choice by reducing the election to essentially a two-party contest and is likely to furnish the major party which has the most public support (even if this is not a majority of votes) with a majority of seats in parliament. Conversely, many of those who support proportional representation do so on the grounds that, by increasing representation from minor parties, it will reduce the ability of major parties to dominate parliament, forcing them into compromises and coalitions.

Where coalition governments are created by a process of bargaining between the parties after a parliament has been elected, the function of making and unmaking governments is to a certain extent removed from the electors and returned to parliament with consequent loss of power by the people. Increasing the independent power of parliament, in this case by giving MPs more opportunity to make and unmake governments, is not necessarily a change towards more democracy. Parliament, of course, is an essential, indeed the central, institution in our democratic system and there are many instances of its powers – for example, the right to question ministers or scrutinize intended legislation – which are clearly means of exerting public pressure on governments. But this is not invariably so. There are certain frequently canvassed reforms of parliament, such as lengthening its term, relaxing party discipline, altering the electoral system to encourage more minor parties and independents, which would certainly increase parliament's power but at the expense of the public rather than on its behalf. Public influence on government does not depend solely on parliament. Equally, if not more, important is the influence exerted through the government's direct appeal to the electorate and its negotiations with interest groups. But these instances of popular power can be frustrated if the government is not able to act and react quickly and cannot count on parliamentary support for its actions. Domination of parliament by one party is thus not necessarily the perversion of democracy or the negation of the people's rights which it is often said to be, particularly by those who take the account of parliament given in constitutional law as a literal account of how parliament ought to function.

However, coalition governments are not necessarily inconsistent with the requirements of the model. Where there are several political parties, each party is under strong pressure during the election campaign to declare its intentions about which other party or parties it will join if elected. Where the potential members of a coalition and the policies they will support have been presented to the voters at an election, the people may still be said to have chosen their government and endorsed its mandate. There are many instances of coalitions providing strong, effective and stable government, particularly in continental Europe where proportional representation is the norm. The English-speaking stereotype of European governments as chronically unstable with endlessly changing coalitions is highly inaccurate.

Moreover, though proportional representation in New Zealand would undoubtedly remove the present bias in favour of major parties, it would not necessarily lead to a proliferation of minor parties in parliament, particularly if there were a 'threshold' or minimum number of votes which a party would need to win in order to gain parliamentary representation (the Royal Commission recommended 4 per cent). Recent levels of support for minor parties, which was as high as 20 per cent in the 1981 and 1984 elections, but fell to 8 per cent in 1987, would not necessarily be repeated in an election held under a form of proportional representation. Many of the votes for minor parties such as the Democrats (formerly Social Credit) or the New Zealand party have been 'protest votes', that is votes cast on the assumption that the party will not win the election or become the government. Supporters of a major party can vote against their party without voting directly for its traditional rival. The purpose is to warn the major parties against being insensitive to the voter's wishes. Significantly, two of the three seats which Social Credit held in recent parliaments were won for the first time at by-elections, occasions when protest voting is more attractive because the question of which party is to govern is not at issue. In spite of the party's claim that its voters are deprived of the representation they have voted for, there is no reason to believe that all those who vote for them are expressing support of their policies or wish to see the Democrats join a government as part of a coalition. Mr Bob Jones, the original leader of the New Zealand party, was quite explicit. His party, which won 12 per cent of the vote in 1984 without gaining a seat, had, in his view, succeeded in its purpose: by drawing votes from National, it had brought down the Muldoon government.

Under a system of proportional representation, where every vote goes towards electing an MP, there is not the same possibility of a negative or protest vote. In this case, support for the existing minor parties, which are products of the existing system, could well dwindle away permanently. It is important to realize that the party system and the pattern of support for different parties is heavily influenced by the existing electoral system. With a radically different electoral system such as proportional representation, both the parties themselves and the voters' choices would also change considerably. In a New Zealand parliament elected on proportional lines, the distribution of seats between parties would probably bear little resemblance to the percentage of votes cast for National, Labour, Democratic, or New Zealand in recent elections. New Zealand does not have the same history of constitutional or religious divisions which led to the existence of a large number of political parties in many of the European countries where proportional representation is used. If the New Zealand people so determined, a strong two-party system could continue under proportional representation.

Our model, with its emphasis on responsive, single-party government, may support an electoral system which treats major parties more favourably than minor parties. It does, however, require that the major parties should compete for public support on equal terms. In this respect, the present system may be somewhat deficient. The number of seats won in parliament, the factor which determines who becomes the government, is not necessarily proportionate to the total number of votes cast for each party. In 1978 Labour gained 40.4 per cent of the total vote compared with National's 39.8 per cent, but National won fifty-one seats compared with Labour's forty. In 1981, Labour again won in terms of total national vote (39 per cent compared with

38.8 per cent for National) but lost the election (forty-three seats compared with National's forty-seven). The reason is that voting support for the two parties is not equally spread across the constituencies. Labour has had a slightly greater share of its votes congregated in very safe seats, but National's votes have been more evenly spread. The representation commission has official observers from both the government and opposition parties present during its deliberations and is no doubt aware of these difficulties, but the 5 per cent degree of tolerance allows it very little room to manœuvre.

The degree of this discrepancy varies according to the pattern of electoral support and the particular five-yearly electoral redistribution of electoral boundaries. It is also complicated by the existence of the Maori roll and Maori voters. Given a greater degree of tolerance, a more equitable result could be engineered, at least on the basis of patterns of support for each party at the last election — 'gerrymandering for democracy' as it has been called. Another alternative would be 'topping up', by reserving a small number of seats to be distributed nationally to the major parties so as to even up the total proportion of votes to seats. Any form of proportional representation would, by definition, give the most seats to the party which wins the most votes. The inequity is at present, perhaps, only minor and affects the result of the election only when support for the two parties is very evenly divided. There is little likelihood that one party could be several percentage points ahead on votes and not win the election. None the less, it is clear that the degree of equity possible between the parties depends on the accidental geographical distribution of their supporters. In theory, at least, the distribution could become much more unbalanced and the inequity intolerable.

Distribution of party support among the various constituencies may also affect the degree of attention given to different sections of voters. Some seats are 'safe' seats: they can usually be counted on to give such overwhelming support to one or other party that, even if the country as a whole swings against the party, these particular seats will be retained. National's safe seats are in rural areas and well-to-do suburbs of the larger cities. Labour's safe seats include the four Maori seats, and city seats with a high concentration of manual and unskilled workers. Parties hoping to win an election do not expect to capture their opponents' safe seats but rather aim to win as many as possible of the 'marginal' seats, those seats where support for the two parties is more evenly balanced. It is a common complaint of voters in safe seats that their votes have no effect on the outcome of the election and are therefore 'wasted'. One of the undoubted advantages of systems of proportional representation is that each vote clearly counts towards the final result. If the parties concentrate their vote-winning efforts on marginal seats, voters who live in marginal seats might be expected to have more indirect power over government than voters in safe seats whose support can either be taken for granted or written off completely.

Marginal seats are certainly objects of more vigorous campaigning. Parties make particular efforts to canvass the whole electorate and get their supporters to the polls on election day. Marginal electorates also receive more visits from other MPs, particularly ministers or potential ministers and the party leaders themselves. However, concrete evidence of favoured treatment for marginal seats and corresponding neglect of safe seats is less easy to find. One instance we have already suggested is the Maori seats, where the neglect of the Maori people and their interests by successive governments can be traced, in part, to the safeness of all four Maori seats; if even one Maori seat had been marginal between National and Labour both parties would surely have paid more attention to the wishes of Maori voters. It is unusual, however, for the members of a particular group or class to be located solely in safe seats; most are spread across marginal and safe seats.

On most issues of government policy it is not possible, without flagrant favouritism, to treat different geographical areas differently. The types of policy which are often used to appeal for support, such as farming subsidies, mortgages for home buyers, family or medical benefits, tax relief and so on, must be applied across the board to all those eligible, whether they live in safe or in marginal seats. Those items of expenditure which can be concentrated in specific localities, such as public works, new schools, hospitals and so on, are usually subject to national priorities closely scrutinized by government departments and by interest groups, who are likely to oppose any attempt to manipulate priorities in favour of marginal constituencies. Indeed, many such decisions have been deliberately removed from direct political control: for instance, priorities for roads and bridges, one of the traditional contents of the 'pork barrel', which governments could use to buy local support, have been placed under a semi-independent statutory board, the National Roads Board. The establishment of state owned enterprises, operating on commercial lines, to replace government departments directly under ministerial control has further reduced the politicians' ability to influence sensitive local decisions, such as railway or post office closures.

Safeness is only a matter of degree and no seat is wholly immune from changing hands. Labour lost one of its traditionally safe seats, Dunedin North, to National in 1975; National lost Ohariu to Labour in 1984. Safe seats, if they do not go over to the opposition, may go to minor parties, especially at by-elections when the choice of government is not usually at stake and voters can afford to be more adventurous. Social Credit (as it then was) won Rangitikei in 1978 and East Coast Bays in 1980, both formerly safe for National. Safe seats are also vulnerable to unofficial, 'alternative' candidates from within the dominant party, seeking to attract traditional supporters away from the sitting member. The continuity of voting patterns is always much more obvious after than before an election, and the parties can rarely afford to take any seat or section of the voters entirely for granted. There is also more to a party's election performance than just the number of seats won. The total number of votes cast throughout the country for each party is also politically significant; so too is the relative swing for or against particular candidates. Loyal party workers in safe seats are equally members of the party as a whole, represented on its regional and national bodies, and their support cannot be taken for granted or their constituencies completely ignored in the eagerness to concentrate on marginals. Thus, though voters in marginal seats certainly have a greater effect on the outcome of elections, there is little evidence that they thereby exercise a disproportionate influence on governments.

The individual MP

According to the model, the main function of the individual MP is to be a member of the parliamentary party team, and to provide his or her own contribution of local knowledge, technical experience and general judgement to the party's total political effort. However, though MPs are party members first and have most of their democratic effect as party members, the other duties they perform as individual representatives provide further avenues for democratic influence on government, and should not be overlooked. In particular, MPs act as individual advocates for local interests or individual constituents. When the focus becomes local and individual, the claims of party recede and MPs are expected to help their constituents regardless of party affiliation. Much of this work involves acting as a referral agent for individual constituents dealing with various public bodies. If the problem concerns a branch of local government, the MP will merely refer the inquirer to the appropriate officer. If it is a matter concerning central government, the MP can take the matter up with the appropriate minister in Wellington. MPs are advocates and trouble-shooters for their constituencies, providing an additional source of access and possible remedy against the government, along with such agencies as the ombudsmen or the courts. For many people, their MP, especially if he or she is known personally, may be more approachable than an anonymous public official or a lawyer.

At the instigation of an MP, a minister may call for an account of what, if anything, departmental officials have done in a particular matter and, by doing so, may uncover an anomaly or administrative injustice or at least provide an explanation for the action taken. MPs act in this way for local bodies in their constituencies and for other institutions such as local schools or industries. Any local group which wishes to exert extra pressure on any section of government will expect its MP to respond to a call for help; several MPs from the same region will often be involved. In pressing for local interests, MPs are expected to, and frequently do, co-operate with their parliamentary neighbours across party lines. The parties themselves recognize that local loyalties may sometimes need to take precedence over party loyalty. A government may decide against allocating a valued resource, such as an upgraded port or new hospital facilities, to a particular town or district. The local MPs, if they are members of the governing party, will have argued strenuously in caucus on behalf of their constituents' case. They will be allowed to disagree publicly with the government decision — one of the few permitted exceptions to the strict rule of party unity.

Not everyone makes equal use of their MP's services in this way; MPs would be inundated with constituency business and would have no time for taking part in committee work or debates if all their constituents approached them when they needed help in their dealings with public bodies. Those with higher levels of education or a greater involvement in community organizations are more likely to know when to approach an MP and also to have the confidence to do so. This non-party, local aspect of the MP's democratic contribution is thus not wholly equal in its effects, and reveals a bias in favour of the well-off and well-educated. None the less, it provides an additional means of making governments responsive to individuals and community interests and thus, though not entirely equal in its operation, may be said to contribute to the overall level of democracy.

On average, MPs give about a third of their time to constituency work when parliament is in session and more when it is adjourned. Motives of public duty (not as uncommon as the public's cynicism about politicians would sometimes suggest) and the natural wish to maintain a favourable public reputation encourage MPs to give careful attention to their constituents. In addition, satisfactory performance of constituency duties may increase their chances of re-election. The electoral sanction works on the MP as an individual as well as on the party as a whole. It might be argued that, if votes are for the party and not the individual, the qualities of the individual candidates, including the degree to which they have nursed their constituencies, will have no bearing on the results. However, not all votes are party votes. Some voters claim to be influenced by the capacity and performance of the candidates and there is always some variation in the relative success of each party in different electorates, or in the same electorates with different candidates. Even if the 'personal' vote is only a few hundred it may make the difference between success and failure in a marginal seat. MPs in marginal seats sometimes therefore spend well over half their time on constituency business.

MPs who are unpopular with their electorates may also run the risk of being unseated by their local party organization or of facing an alternative candidate, unofficially claiming affiliation with their own party. This is more likely in safe seats where selection is particularly sought after and there is less risk that a party split will let the opposing party win. In the 1978 election, for example, two National MPs faced alternative National candidates. In 1981 a senior and well-respected cabinet minister, Mr Allan Highet, faced a vigorous, though ultimately unsuccessful, campaign to deny him nomination and almost certain re-election for Remuera. Since 1978, three National MPs have been denied renomination. Vulnerability to local unpopularity is particularly strong in the National party, which allows a high degree of local autonomy in the choice of candidates. Labour's selection procedure gives a more important role to the central party, sufficient, for instance, to prevent the renomination of Mr Gerald O'Brien, MP for Island Bay, in 1978, when he had considerable local support. The party leadership can thus offer some protection to MPs facing local challengers for the party's nomination, as it did for Mrs Mary Batchelor, long-standing MP for Avon, when she was challenged in 1984.

We have argued that the electoral sanction, the MP's fear of losing the next election, is the single most important means by which the people can influence government action through exerting pressure on MPs. The effect of this sanction extends over much of an MP's activity, as astute members will be constantly on the watch for matters which may affect their popularity with the electorate and their chances at the next election. There are no issues which are inherently unpolitical; any issue, however apparently uncontroversial, can become the subject of political controversy at any time. None the less, among the mass of business considered by MPs, many items appear to have no electoral consequences and the MP is free to judge them 'on the merits of the case'. This applies particularly to business conducted in select committees, where proposed legislation or departmental administration is often discussed in a comparatively non-partisan and cooperative atmosphere. Here, even an opposition MP can suggest improvements which may be accepted by the minister and his officials. In these non-controversial, non-political discussions and decisions, can the members of the public exert any influence or are the MPs entirely free of democratic control?

In so far as politicians are free of pressure or obligation to follow public opinion in any way in this area, there is no clear popular influence upon them. On the other hand, there is a sense in which a member of parliament can represent the wishes or opinions of his or her constituents without knowing what they actually want or think. This can occur if the MP is literally or typically representative of them, if he or she personally exemplifies their typical attitudes, background and values and can therefore be expected to think and act as they would. To the extent that certain sections of the population are over-represented in parliament — males, the over-forties, the better educated — these sections may be able to exert more influence on government decision-making; or, if no influence is actually exerted from outside parliament, these groups can at least be said to have their points of view more frequently endorsed by MPs. Ideally, from this point of view, a democratic parliament would be a typical cross-section of the electorate, in which all sections of opinion were equally represented.

However, the democratic activities of the representative we have discussed so far do not depend on politicians being typically representative of their constituents. They involve a different sense of representation, where one person represents others by acting for them or on their behalf, like an agent or advocate. In those areas of government activity covered by the sanction of political publicity and electoral success or failure what is needed in the politician is the ability to judge what will please or displease the voters. One does not have to be a pensioner to gauge the political reactions of pensioners, or a farmer to perceive the political demands of farmers. Belonging to the group in question may help to provide additional understanding of their wishes, but does not guarantee it. Equally, if not more, reliable are the broad sympathy and practical judgement which the skilled politician can bring to the assessment of the wishes and likely reactions of many different sections of the voting public.

The fact that most politicians are male and over forty does not mean that all decisions are necessarily made in the interests of this minority.

To be so self-interested would spell electoral suicide for a governing party which must always be on the watch for any potential group of electoral support, whether or not these groups are actually represented in the governing caucus. However, in those less controversial areas where political sanctions do not extend and where members are more free to judge 'on the merits of the case', personal background and attitudes will be more influential. Here, the viewpoints of under-represented groups, such as women or the under-forties, are likely to receive less than their due share of attention. An ideally democratic parliament would, therefore, be one consisting of skilled and experienced politicians, capable of responding to actual and potential demands from the public on matters likely to have political or electoral consequences, and yet containing an accurate cross-section of opinions and occupations in order to represent the public adequately in non-controversial, non-political aspects of government business. This ideal combination may be unattainable. Without wishing to justify the representative imbalance found in the New Zealand (and other) parliaments, we may agree that the role of 'agent' is democratically more important than that of the representative as 'typical example'. The former deals with those issues which are electorally significant and therefore of most concern to the voters. If we have to choose, it is more important that MPs should be able to act effectively in their constituents' interests than that they be typically representative of them.

But do voters really have much say in who becomes their MP? MPs may be finally appointed by their constituents at an election, but, given the importance of party identification in elections, it is the initial adoption by the party which determines who is elected. How democratic is the selection of candidates? All parties see candidate selection as a matter concerning members of the party only. Candidates themselves must be formal members of the party, though only Labour requires a period of membership before nomination can be accepted. All members of the party in a particular constituency can be involved in the process of selection, though usually the final decision is made by representatives elected by the rank and file rather than by a direct ballot of all members. Labour gives almost equal rights to the central as distinct from the local party organization. National officially leaves the final decision to the constituency members though national officers vet the list of applicants. Both parties obviously aim to choose candidates who will make effective and popular politicians. The preferences of the electorate as a whole, therefore, have some indirect influence over who is selected, even if only a few actually make the selection.

Candidate selection could be opened up to a wider group, to a poll of all party members or even to all interested voters, as in the system of election primaries used widely in the United States. Such procedures certainly involve more people in the process of candidate selection. Especially for those living in constituencies traditionally safe for one party, a poll of all voters on who is to stand for that party would give everyone a real say in who represents them in Wellington. On the other hand, a danger of the primary system is that the field of potential candidates may be narrowed rather than widened. Public election campaigns require canvassing and advertising. Success by an individual in an election without party support will often depend on considerable personal expenditure, beyond the reach of those without personal wealth or the backing of wealthy supporters.

Free votes and referendums

On questions such as liquor licensing and abortion, party discipline is removed and MPs are required to make a 'free' vote, based on their own personal judgement. The motives of politicians in providing free votes are easy to comprehend. Traditionally, such votes have tended to be on matters of personal morality, often linked with the teaching of certain churches (Roman Catholics on abortion, some Protestant churches on gambling and liquor). Divisions on these issues cut right across traditional party lines. The parties, based mainly on socio-economic divisions with principles appropriate to the economic and occupational groups which give them greatest support, cannot take a stand without deeply offending an important and vocal section of their supporters. They therefore happily support the free vote as a means of avoiding involvement in disputes which could seriously threaten the unity of their parties and cause loss of support at the polls. Their instinct for self-preservation may appear cowardly but can be justified in terms of preserving a strong two-party system. New Zealand has been comparatively free from openly sectarian conflict in politics, and few, would wish to encourage the development of new political divisions along religious lines.

However, though the parties may have good reason to abdicate responsibility on such issues, they should find alternative democratic means of allowing the public to have their say. The free vote is not satisfactory because, in a system of party government, it temporarily removes MPs from the pressure of electoral accountability. The recent debates about abortion and homosexual law, both highly salient and controversial issues, illustrate these difficulties. Some MPs have tried to follow the views of their constituents by, for example, taking polls among their constituents. Others have taken positions calculated to win favour, or avoid disfavour, with the various abortion pressure groups in their constituencies. In a free vote public accountability is difficult to establish. MPs may be subject to intense personal pressure for a time, but it is not readily translated into electoral profit or loss. As most voters vote at elections on party lines, attitudes of individual MPs on non-party questions can affect only a small percentage of votes. The highly organized pro- and anti-abortion lobbies tried to induce voters in the 1978 and 1981 elections to vote for candidates sympathetic to their views on abortion. But the election results do not appear to have been significantly affected by the candidates' stand on this issue. Similarly, individual results in the 1987 election were not noticeably affected by the issue of homosexual law reform, in spite of the high degree of public controversy it had aroused in 1985 and 1986.

Some justifications of free votes make a positive virtue of the lack of accountability. They treat such 'moral' questions as abortion, liquor, gambling and capital punishment as 'conscience' issues, where MPs should be able to follow the dictates of their consciences, in the knowledge that their electoral chances are very unlikely to be affected by the stand they take. It is one thing, however, to allow that MPs may use their own judgement in those humdrum or uncontroversial areas of government activity where the light of political publicity does not usually penetrate; it is quite another to advocate the use of free votes in matters where the glare of publicity shines only too brightly. To do so is to attempt to reduce the degree of democratic control over parliamentary decisions. The appropriate democratic method of deciding issues which the parties avoid is not the free vote but the referendum. And referendums have been used in New Zealand for just this type of moral issue — for example, gambling (the establishment of the TAB in 1949), and liquor (the referendums on liquor hours in 1949 and 1967 as well as the regular triennial vote on prohibition continuance or state control).

There are a number of practical objections raised against referendums. They can be expensive to mount; the precise question to be put to the electorate needs to be carefully worded, and there is no guarantee that the government will not use its control over the administration of referendums to frame the question in a vague or slanted direction; there is also the problem of turnout – if only a small proportion of the voters bother to vote, the decision will not reflect public opinion but will be determined by vociferous minority groups. Most of these difficulties can be surmounted. Problems of expense can be minimized by holding several referendums at once, or by combining them with a general election. This may also solve the problem of securing a reasonable turnout, if a question which has aroused comparatively little public interest is coupled with a more controversial question or with a general election. In 1967 the holding of a referendum on licensing hours – a question of considerable public interest – was taken as an opportunity to ask the electorate's opinion on extending the term of parliament, an issue which would not have raised a very large turnout on its own. Similarly, the referendums on liquor licensing which accompany each general election receive a far greater response than they would if held independently. The problem of finding the right question remains substantial, but on most issues a reasonably unambiguous and fair-minded option or set of options is possible. The chance that a government might be tempted to put a loaded question to a referendum and risk considerable public uproar is hardly sufficient reason for ruling out the holding of a referendum altogether.

The main reason for objecting to referendums and preferring free votes as a means of deciding non-party issues is often not so much the practical difficulties of a referendum, as a general mistrust of public opinion as an appropriate judge of such matters. It is commonly said for instance, that capital punishment would never have been abolished or certainly not abolished when it was, if the decision had been left to public opinion. Whatever the strength of this objection to public opinion, a question which will be considered in the concluding chapter, it should at least be clear that the preference for non-party, free votes over party votes or referendum decisions is a preference for a lesser degree of democracy. Free votes frustrate the accountability to the voters which the parties provide indirectly through their competition for electoral support, and which referendums provide more directly. The call for more free votes and a consequent reduction of party discipline and party voting, like the call for a longer parliamentary term, reflects a preference for greater independence of MPs from public pressure and consequently for a reduction in the democratic control of government. Unfortunately, the anti-democratic tendency of a more independent and free-voting parliament is masked by official constitutional theory and symbolism. Among the formal elements of the constitution, that is the Crown (the governor-general), the ministers of the Crown, the judiciary and parliament, it is parliament which, being elected by the people, is taken to represent the people's will. A free and unfettered parliament is seen as a guarantee of a free and independent people. Conversely, any attempt to interfere with parliament's freedom is an attempt to circumscribe the people's rights.

Parliamentary procedure treats MPs as independent individuals (it is a breach of standing orders to suggest that an MP is acting under orders from someone outside the House), and implies that an ideal parliament is a free-voting assembly of individual members. There is thus a strong traditional and symbolic connection between the independence of parliament and the democratic rights of citizens. Democracy appears to be compromised by the curbs on MPs' independence imposed by political parties. It should have become clear, however, that an independent parliament does not necessarily enhance the democratic control of government. External pressure on parliament from the electorate, relayed by political parties, is a means of increasing, not frustrating, the citizens' power over government.

In terms of our model, the central function of parliament is competition between the two major parties for the support of the voters at elections. A number of factors suggest that the people exercise a considerable degree of power in this way: the flexibility and electoral sensitivity of both major parties; the amount of detailed policy specified in election programmes; the relative frequency of elections; the high turnout of voters at elections. On the other hand, there are areas where parliament is less than equal in its effect: the complexities and anomalies of the Maori electorates; the tendency of the better educated and more wealthy to make greater use of the services of their individual MPs; moreover, though elections place considerable limits on a government's freedom of action, there are great areas of public policy and administration into which this type of political influence hardly penetrates at all. Still to be discussed, however, are other channels of democratic power besides parliament and the electoral process which may help to redress the balance.

FOUR: The interest group system

Interest groups and corporatism

The interest group system includes all the various groups whose members share a common interest or a common concern, and who combine and organize among themselves to influence government decisions and public policy in their favour. Interest-group influence can be exerted at many different points of government and by a variety of techniques. Sometimes the pressure is aimed at a particular government department. If the matter is a minor one and handled by a subordinate official, the representatives of the interest group will often make a direct approach to that official or the official's immediate superiors. If it is more important or contentious, the point of contact will be senior public servants or ministers themselves. Alternatively, some areas of public policy may not be in the direct control of the minister or his or her department, but may have been delegated to an independent public body such as a corporation, statutory board or advisory committee. In such cases the group may make direct representations to this body and may indeed have representatives who are members of it. Again, groups may have recourse to parliament. The interest group and parliamentary systems are closely interrelated. All public bodies, whether government departments or statutory bodies, are to some degree answerable to parliament. MPs, either as individuals or on behalf of their parties, may take up the cause of a particular group, and may ask questions of the appropriate minister or press for changes in enabling legislation on the group's behalf.

First, some general problems of definition. What is to count as an interest group? What, if any, is the difference between 'interest' groups and 'pressure' groups? The appropriate method is to construct a model or 'ideal' type, which different instances may approach to a greater or lesser extent. The ideal interest group would probably have the following features: membership open to all who share the interest in question; representatives and officers of the group appointed by the members; a federal structure consisting of constituent branches and a national organization; provision for regular contact with government officials and politicians. Within these general guidelines great variation is possible. Some interest groups are large institutions which employ sizeable professional staffs; others are run almost entirely on voluntary labour. Some are permanent organizations which exist for generations, and others come into existence and later disband or wither away. The type of interest which is pursued may differ. Some interest groups, including most of the more powerful ones, are formed for the members of a particular occupation and are concerned with pursuing the interests of those engaged in that occupation. Others may be quite altruistic in their motive, working on behalf of others, such as the handicapped or orphans; yet others, such as environmentalists or peace groups, may be concerned with a particular cause or type of issue rather than with a group of people.

Neither 'interest group' nor 'pressure group' is an entirely appropriate term. The objection to 'pressure group' is that it suggests one particular method of exerting influence, through direct confrontation, backed up by the threat of sanctions. It may also connote undue or illegitimate influence, which would be misleading when governments openly and properly consult and co-operate with groups and treat them as the legitimate advocates of their members' interests. The main reason for preferring 'interest group' is therefore to emphasize that consultation with interested parties is politically legitimate. On the other hand, 'interest group' may suggest a concentration on the immediate interests of the members of the group, and may appear to exclude other, less self-interested groups, concerned about a wider cause or public issue. There is a common, academic distinction between 'interest' or 'occupational' groups, which pursue the interests of an occupational group or class, and 'cause' or 'issue' groups, which campaign on some public cause or issue. In this study, 'interest group' will be used in a looser and more extended sense including any group with a common political aim or interest, whether this interest is that of members of the same occupation or of those who support a particular public cause.

The close connection between government and interest groups is often associated with a 'corporatist' theory of the state. Corporatism is a concept of broad meaning which has been associated at different times with both socialism and fascism but is now increasingly used, in the context of western industrial democracies, to describe a form of government in which power lies with organized interest groups rather than with elected political leaders or public servants. According to this corporatist model, public policy is decided by officially recognized interest groups, or public 'corporations', each of which is allowed a monopoly of authority within its own sector. Decisions on matters which concern more than one interest are made by negotiation between the groups concerned. The state, that is the central political organ of government, confers authority on the sectional organizations by recognizing them as the sole legitimate representatives of their respective interests. It provides the focus for their negotiations and enforces the decisions which they reach. But it does not otherwise attempt to interfere in their internal decisions or impose its own views on the agreements they may make with one another. Though corporatism implies government by interest groups, not all types of interest group government are properly corporatist. Corporatism involves not only placing power in the hands of groups, but also 'incorporating' them into government by conferring public status and authority on them. Other theories of interest group politics, particularly those associated with the pluralist approach to politics prevalent in the United States, do not emphasize any public or legal status conferred on groups. Instead, the political system is seen as an open market-place, like the market of *laissez-faire* economics, where privately organized groups compete for political influence, while retaining their private status as collections of citizens independent of the government.

In New Zealand the most obvious corporatist tendency has been the establishment of statutory bodies, such as public corporations, boards and other 'quangos'. Such bodies are created by, or under, the authority of statutes which remove the area of activity from direct, day-to-day control by the government. They commonly include representatives of recognized interest groups. Historically, the preference for control by statutory boards or public corporations was associated more with the National party and its predecessors, while the Labour party preferred direct, ministerial control through government departments. Subsequently, both parties have equally supported the establishment of relatively independent public bodies. Interest group activity in New Zealand is not wholly corporatist in nature. The private *laissez-faire* type is also evident, particularly in the way that new groups arise to press for a particular cause or to protest against some aspect of government policy. A familiar pattern has been for groups to start off as purely private, and then become gradually accepted as part of the formal structure of government consultation. Under the Lange Labour government, following international trends, there has been a move away from formal corporatist consultation of interest groups and a corresponding increase in the informal influence of private groups, particularly from the business sector.

In terms of our democratic model, the interest group system helps to share political power among the people. As with the parliamentary system, much of the power is exercised indirectly, through anticipated reactions at various stages and levels of decision-making. Most rank and file members of particular groups will do little more than pay an annual subscription, perhaps attend an occasional meeting at a time of crisis, or vote to elect representatives if elections are contested. However, if they are aware of their own interests as members of the group and are prepared to become more active if their representatives are unsuccessful in securing what they want, this will often be sufficient to guarantee responsiveness not only from their representatives but also from the various branches of government which deal with their group. In assessing the degree of democracy provided by the interest group system, it is necessary to assess the extent to which different interests are effectively represented and whether they all receive consideration in proportion to the number of people they represent. We also need to follow the principle arrived at in our earlier discussion of political equality in a pluralist society: that, where a number of people share the same interest, each will exercise the same degree of power; where different groups of people have different degrees of interest in an issue, the degree of power exercised by members of each group should vary accordingly.

The interest group system in New Zealand has not been the subject of much detailed research. Compared with the excitement of parliament and the electoral contest, interest group politics seem tedious and tame. It does not often make the news or attract the attention of commentators and students. Significantly, the protest groups, the groups which rely most heavily on media publicity and public demonstrations for their impact, have received a disproportionate amount of academic exposure. But these groups, though important, are exceptions to the norm; most interest groups usually work quietly and effectively through well-established channels of political consultation and influence. This network of consultation, largely undescribed and unanalysed, provides what is in many ways the key to understanding the distribution of political power in this country. To gain some understanding of how the interest group system has worked, we will examine the operation of interest groups within one particular area of government activity.

Farmer interest groups

The example selected is agriculture, by general agreement the most important sector of the New Zealand economy, at least for export earnings, and in many ways the most efficient. With certain minor exceptions, agricultural property is in private hands and farming is not a state-owned or state-operated industry. However, there are many areas in which government and farming impinge on one another. Government agencies give considerable help to the farming industry, for instance in marketing and academic research. Governments have also given direct subsidies for such items as fertilizers, stock retention and supplementary prices for farming products. Farmers also make demands in other areas of government activity, such as health and education in country areas, or general economic management, including the need to lower inflation and prevent the rising cost of goods and services which the farmer must buy. To meet these political needs, there has arisen a complex set of relationships between farming interest groups, government departments and statutory boards.

Most of the farmers' interest groups are combined within the organization known as the Federated Farmers of New Zealand. Federated Farmers is a 'peak association', a federation of a number of formally independent farmers' groups, with different sectional and regional interests. Its organization is deliberately complex, in order to accommodate these different interests. First, it is divided regionally into twenty-two localities or 'provinces', each with its own officers, executive, and regular meetings as well as an annual conference. Within each province, there are a number of branches, about 500 in total throughout the country. Secondly, it is divided into a general organization, which deals with problems affecting all sections of the farming industry, and special produce sections dealing with different types of farming. The three main sections are Dairy, Meat and Wool, and Agriculture (including wheat and other types of cropping). A farmer who joins Federated Farmers joins a local branch, and opts for one of the produce sections. A farmer whose farming is evenly divided between different types of farming may belong to more than one section. Membership is voluntary and runs at around 30,000 or about 85 per cent of those eligible to join.

Both the general organization and the produce sections have their own, separate institutions. Both are organized on a provincial and a national ('dominion') basis, each with its own provincial and dominion conferences to determine general policy and elect officials. At the national level, there is a dominion council of about fifty members which meets quarterly. There are also dominion office-holders, such as a president and vice-presidents, and a dominion executive which meets at least once a month. Each produce section also has its own dominion council and executive. The broad general policy of the

Federation is formally decided by the annual conference, voting on remits proposed by individual provinces or the dominion council. More specific policy is decided by the council at its quarterly meetings. Regular formal support from the rank and file and their representatives is vital if the executive is to maintain authority and effectiveness.

One reason for the success of Federated Farmers is its combination of autonomy and liaison. Each produce section is entitled to act independently on any matter which affects its interests alone and does not impinge on the interests of other sections. Thus, a question concerning dairy farmers only will be discussed at provincial meetings of the dairy section, and then taken up by the dominion council of the dairy section whose chairman will have direct contact with the appropriate government official or department. The general organization would not attempt to interfere at any point with this process. Federated Farmers as a whole will act only on matters which concern all farmers — matters such as taxation, interest rates, transport costs and so on. At the same time, if the organization as a whole is to be an effective voice of all farmers, it must keep in touch with the specific as well as the general concerns of all farmers. Thus, though there is no central control or direction, there is considerable liaison at all levels between the sections and the general organization. For instance, the three chairmen of the produce sections are all members of the dominion executive of Federated Farmers. At the provincial level, the executive meetings are attended by a representative of each produce section. Similarly, the provincial president of Federated Farmers is ex officio a member of the provincial executive of each produce section.

In these and other ways, the office-bearers and committee members of the different parts of the organization keep in touch with each other and with each other's concerns. Possible conflict between different sections or regions can be anticipated and softened. Such conflict is not infrequent. Dairy farmers and sheep farmers, for instance, have long-standing differences about the degree of co-operative and public control of farming, with dairy farmers more ready to accept collective methods of production and marketing and sheep farmers more jealously cherishing their independence and supporting a free enterprise approach to farming. There are also specific conflicts between, for example, grain growers looking for a good return from their crops and pig and poultry farmers wanting cheap feed. In such cases, the general organization of Federated Farmers has seen its role as representing all farmers and seeking a middle way between its more vociferous factions; its leaders have, therefore, tended to be conciliatory rather than aggressive in style and temperament.

To help provide a united voice for the farming community, Federated Farmers is officially affiliated with other related farming groups, such as the Federation of Young Farmers Clubs and smaller producer associations such as the Tobacco Growers' Federation and the National Beekeepers' Association. In general, one cannot but be impressed by the degree of interest organization in the farming industry. Every local or special interest has its own organization and representatives who can speak effectively for its members. At the same time, the federal structure, with its overlapping memberships and regular liaison, allows support to be mobilized for any common interest shared by several sections of the industry.

Such a large and manifold organization can interact with government in a great variety of ways. Each year, for instance, Federated Farmers makes its own submissions to the minister of finance on what it would like to see in the budget for the following year. It also expects to be involved in discussions with government on broad economic policy, such as taxation and monetary policy. Within the farming sector, its influence is naturally more pervasive. Any new development in government farming policy will be discussed, as a matter of course, with the appropriate representatives from Federated Farmers. Because Federated Farmers is so effective both in articulating the differing viewpoints in the farming industry and in forming an acceptable consensus between them, ministers of agriculture tend to rely on its advice as representative of farming opinion.

In this respect the leadership of Federated Farmers walks a tightrope. Its close relations with government and the trust in which it is held by ministers depend on its ability to reconcile differences within the farming community, and on its willingness to compromise in the face of other conflicting points of view put forward by the government or by other sections of the community. On the other hand, its effectiveness also depends on its remaining representative of the views of its ordinary members, who will not be slow to criticize their leaders if they appear to be weak or to be selling out to other interests. In their dealings with government, the leaders of Federated Farmers may need to remind politicians and public servants that, if a satisfactory deal is not forthcoming, the issue can be made public and political opposition aroused. An occasional public outburst helps to preserve this bargaining power. Ministers will also need to be reminded that, if Federated Farmers is unsuccessful in pursuing the interests of farmers it may be outflanked by a more militant and troublesome organization, such as the Sheep and Cattlemen's Association, a rebel group of sheep farmers, which was formed to oppose the compulsory acquisition of wool in the early 1970s. In return for favourable treatment, the various councillors, chairmen and executive members of Federated Farmers will undertake to explain to their members the conflicting pressures operating on the government and will try to win consent for any concessions farmers have had to make.

Federated Farmers as a whole was under particular strain in the first years of the Lange Labour government. The farming sector suffered a serious economic recession as major subsidies were abolished, interest rates rose, and a more valuable New Zealand dollar made exports less competitive internationally. Should farmers fight for the restoration of subsidies and for government intervention to lower interest and exchange rates? Or should they accept the general deregulation of the economy and the move to greater reliance on market forces and instead press for the extension of this policy to other sectors, particularly manufacturing and the public sector as a means of reducing farmers' costs and 'equalizing the pain'? The Federation leadership favoured the latter approach, recognizing that a return to the previous levels of government intervention was politically unlikely. Many of the rank and file members, however, particularly those who were heavily mortgaged, criticized what they saw as their leaders' meek acceptance of an economic policy which would permanently damage farming in New Zealand. The leaders faced a number of very stormy local meetings before their policy was eventually accepted. Farmers in South Canterbury publicly slaughtered and buried sheep rather than send them to the meat works for no profit, action which provoked a negative public reaction and was disowned by the Federation leadership. However, the Federation did agree to an action campaign in 1986, culminating in a mass march on parliament. While accepting the need for market-led prices, the Federation pressed hard for transitional help for farmers caught with high levels of debt. In the event, the long-awaited farm package in 1986 gave little direct relief. It was described as a 'lemon' by the president of Federated Farmers who reminded the Labour government of its need to retain parliamentary seats in provincial areas dependent on farming.

Within the farming sector, much use has been made of statutory boards, advisory committees and other public bodies as means of incorporating the views of representative interest groups into the making and administration of public policy. They form an alternative method of consulting interested parties. The more constitutionally orthodox practice is for the cabinet or ministers to consult interested parties informally and then take the final decision themselves, being responsible for this decision to parliament. The establishment of a statutory body, however, increases the independence and status of interest groups, formalizing their participation in the decision-making process at the same time as reducing detailed accountability to parliament. Statutory bodies operate under legislation (or, in some cases, government regulation) which determines their sphere of competence and specifies their membership. The powers of some bodies are quite circumscribed. Advisory committees, such as the Apiary Advisory Committee or the Artificial Insemination Advisory Committee, may be charged with merely tendering advice to the government about some particular aspect of agriculture. But the statutory powers of other bodies, including the large producer boards, such as the Dairy Board and the Meat Board, are very considerable, enabling the collection and disbursement of millions of dollars annually and delegating control over a large section of the country's export production. These bodies are accountable to parliament through the minister, and parliament is free to alter or rescind their empowering legislation. But the minister does not have responsibility for the day-to-day running of their affairs and they are not subject to the same degree of political supervision as government departments. Their staffs are not public servants and they are free from many of the controls which Treasury and the State Services Commission exercise over government departments.

As the main farmers' interest group, Federated Farmers nominates representatives to nearly forty public bodies. These include such obviously agricultural bodies as the Agricultural Pests Destruction Council and the Rural Banking and Finance Corporation, and also more wide-ranging organizations such as the Standards Association of New Zealand, the Queen Elizabeth II National Trust and the Pacific Basin Economic Council. Membership of statutory bodies is usually carefully representative of the various interested parties. The National Hydatids Council, for instance, consists of an officer of the Ministry of Agriculture and Fisheries, an officer of the Department of Health, nominees of Federated Farmers, the New Zealand Local Government Association, the New Zealand Kennel Club, the Federation of Young Farmers Clubs, the New Zealand Veterinary Association, and the New Zealand Institute of Hydatids Control Officers.

Within the portfolio of the minister of agriculture, there are fifty-seven statutory boards, councils, authorities, corporations and committees. The most important are the major producer boards, the Meat, Dairy, Wool, and Apple and Pear Boards. These boards provide additional opportunities for the representation of farmers' interests. The Meat Board, for instance, consists of nine members, of whom two are appointed by the government, one by the Dairy Board, and the other six by meat producers through an electoral committee made up of twenty-five regional representatives and one representative of the Meat and Wool Council of Federated Farmers. The basic function of the electoral committee is to appoint people to fill vacancies on the Board. But the committee also meets twice a year to discuss matters which are under consideration by the Board. It thus provides a further means of keeping the Meat Board in touch with producers' concerns and attitudes, separate from, though complementary to, the representative structure of Federated Farmers. In addition, the Meat Board has regular meetings with government officials and with the Meat and Wool Council of Federated Farmers. An example of how these interpenetrating organizations co-ordinate their approaches to government can be found in a routine announcement from the president of Federated Farmers in 1979:

The four producer boards — Meat, Wool, Dairy, and Apple and Pear — met with Federated Farmers on 31 January for initial discussions on the industry's attitude to the minimum supplementary prices scheme introduced in last year's Budget. From these discussions and from those which the Meat and Wool and Dairy Councils [of Federated Farmers] will be having at their meetings this week, this month's Dominion Council will work out a policy to be discussed in the provinces over the next few months. (*Straight Furrow* 9 February 1979)

The tendency towards corporatism, that is the delegation of public policy formulation to officially recognized interest groups, becomes apparent when parliament considers amendments to the legislation under which statutory boards must act or which regulate some area of agricultural production. In 1980 parliament considered twelve amendments to statutes within the agricultural portfolio, many of them concerned with the powers and structure of statutory bodies. In all cases the proposed legislation had been discussed with the appropriate interest groups; indeed, the original initiative had often come from the groups themselves. Wherever possible, the agreement of all parties was secured before the bill was introduced. For instance, the Apiaries Amendment Bill provided an updating of the Apiaries Act, broadening the definition of honey to cover honeydew, simplifying the inspection process and allowing greater control of export standards. The amendment had been discussed with the National Beekeepers Association, the New Zealand Honey Marketing Authority and the Beech Honeydew Producers Association, all of whom supported the proposal. Similarly, the Apple and Pear Marketing Amendment Bill recommended changes in the levy system supporting the financial operations of the Board, and had been asked for by the Board itself.

It had been discussed by the Ministry of Agriculture with the Board, the Fruitgrowers Federation and many apple growers.

On more routine matters, the discussion will have been conducted by the minister and his officials; on more important or more contentious issues, the minister may enlist the support of a caucus committee. Thus the Milk Amendment Bill, which introduced significant changes in the membership of the Milk Board, and the Poultry Bill, which involved the amalgamation of the Poultry Board and the Egg Marketing Authority, were handled by sub-committees of the government caucus agriculture committee. But the same pattern of exhaustive prior consultation emerges. The caucus sub-committee on the town milk industry received 193 submissions from interested parties; it produced a report which was then further discussed by the main interest groups before the proposed legislation was finally drafted. Similarly, the caucus sub-committee on the poultry industry recommended that the Poultry Board and the Egg Marketing Authority be amalgamated, after the change had been requested by the members of the industry and the two bodies concerned. The sub-committee included the proposal in its review paper on the industry which was then made available to the interested parties for discussion and comment.

In the elaborate process of decision-making by the various interests in the farming industry, government provides the formal structure within which the various recognized interests operate; it also, when necessary, implements the decisions that are made. But, to a considerable degree, it does not attempt to impose its own point of view on the various interests. There is wide acceptance that sectional interest groups should be left to settle their own affairs. This is illustrated by the reactions of the opposition to legislation introduced by the minister of agriculture after consultation with the interested parties. Normally, one would expect the opposition to criticize any government proposal. However, if the interest groups are in clear agreement, the opposition warmly welcomes the legislation. Indeed, it vies with the government in congratulating that area of the farming industry on its efficiency and value to the community. This was the case in 1980, for example, with the Wool Testing Authority Amendment Bill and the Veterinary Services Amendment Bill which the opposition supported without reservation. Moreover, where the opposition does criticize, their criticisms are not usually to do with the substance of the proposal; rather they claim that the consultation process has been deficient in some way or other. For instance, the Tobacco Growers Amendment Bill, which proposed measures to deal with a surplus production of tobacco leaf, was introduced at the request of the Tobacco Board (a

113

body representing all interested parties in the production and marketing of tobacco). But it was clear that not all interests represented on the Board supported the proposal. The Tobacco Growers Federation, in particular, made submissions seeking to have the proposal amended. Their case was vigorously taken up by the opposition, whose leader, Mr Rowling, included many tobacco growers among his local constituents. The point at issue was whether the interests of one of the main parties had been given sufficient weight in the discussions and in the eventual proposal. Debate in parliament thus provides a further forum for those groups not satisfied with the earlier attempt at consensus.

The opposition may also take up the issue of whether all relevant groups have received official recognition. For instance, the newly constituted Milk Board, proposed by the Milk Amendment Bill, allowed for two members representing the milk vendors to be nominated by the Dominion Federation of Milk Vendors. In submissions made to the caucus committee which conducted the original inquiry, and then in subsequent submissions to the parliamentary select committee, an alternative group of milk vendors, the National Union of Milk Vendors, claimed a right to membership of the Board. They claimed to represent 20 per cent of milk vendors in the country and their case was taken up by the opposition. The government, however, resisted on the grounds that the Federation was the major and most representative organization of milk vendors, more responsible and less troublesome than the rival union. The same pattern, with the opposition taking up the cause of a disgruntled group, occurred in discussion of the Poultry Board Bill. This bill provided for five representatives of poultry producers who were to be selected from five regional associations of poultry farmers by an electoral process which the minister of agriculture would administer. However, the newly formed Dominion Poultry Farmers Federation, claiming to represent 40 per cent of the country's poultry farmers, sought the right to nominate directly to the Board itself and was supported by the opposition. Its case was rejected by the caucus committee and the government, again on the grounds that the Federation was insufficiently representative and responsible.

In all these cases, we see the politics of interest group competition and negotiation being extended into the parliamentary arena. But the parliamentary debate has tended to be conducted within the same corporatist assumptions that underlie the bulk of interest group activity which never becomes the subject of parliamentary debate: the task of government is not to impose its own view of what should be done, but to make sure that all decisions are arrived at after proper consultation of legitimately interested parties and represent a reasonable and equitable consensus which should be acceptable to all parties. There may, on occasion, be room for argument about who should be recognized as one of the legitimate interest groups and about whether the final decision is fair and acceptable; but it is taken for granted that these are the general principles which ought to be followed.

An interesting example of the interest group system under stress is provided by the attempt to impose compulsory wool acquisition on the sheep farming industry in the early 1970s. Unlike the longer-established Dairy and Meat Boards, which are closely involved in the marketing of dairy and meat exports respectively, the Wool Board has not had such powers and wool has traditionally been marketed through a system of public auction. During the 1960s, particularly as the international market for wool became depressed, there were moves to make the Wool Board more responsible for marketing. In 1971 the Wool Board proposed the setting up of a wool marketing authority which would aim eventually to market all wool processed in New Zealand. The scheme was submitted to the Meat and Wool Section of Federated Farmers where it received general support. Under pressure from the government, however, the proposal was revised to require compulsory acquisition of all wool immediately rather than eventually. The 1972 annual conference of the Meat and Wool Section still supported the proposal in this amended and more radical form, though many woolgrowers were clearly unhappy about it.

Opposition groups sprang up in several sheep farming regions and quickly formed themselves into the New Zealand Woolgrowers Action Committee. They set out to demonstrate that the Meat and Wool Section did not truly represent sheep farmers' opinions and to block the legislation planned for the parliamentary session of 1972. This opposition was eventually successful, partly through the accident of rising prices for wool which lessened the pressure for reform. The Action Committee lobbied the parliamentary lands and agriculture committee and individual MPs. It was election year and MPs from sheep farming areas, overwhelmingly National, were understandably nervous about a proposal which might lose them electoral support; the Labour opposition did not hesitate to highlight the conflict between the government and its traditional rural supporters.

This episode illustrates a number of features about interest group activity. The regular channels of communication had failed to reflect their members' views accurately. The costs of such failure would be substantial in terms of diminished standing for Federated Farmers within the farming community and strained personal relations within

115

a group where many are known personally to each other and where easy, friendly relations are the valued norm. Such an incident serves to remind the farming representatives that they cannot afford to get out of touch with their members or take their support for granted. If the potential for such damaging intra-industry conflict is always present, there is a strong incentive to anticipate it by consulting adequately beforehand. The fact that such outbreaks are rare is thus more likely to indicate that the process of consultation is working adequately, and need not imply that the leadership is never questioned by a quiescent rank and file.

The episode also demonstrates how the interest group system interacts with the rest of the political system. It shows, for instance, how the government does not always act merely as an arbiter of interest group negotiation, but is sometimes involved itself as one of the interested parties with its own preferred policy which it wishes to see implemented, in this case immediate, compulsory acquisition. That it failed ultimately in this instance illustrates the difficulty of imposing a policy against the determined opposition of an organised interest. Finally, it shows how parliament can be an alternative channel of interest group influence, if the normal channels are insensitive to the wishes of a group. So long as the interest groups represent their members' demands and receive a reasonable amount of attention from government and other groups, the system is likely to carry on without any apparent political influence from parliament. But if there is conflict and one group or interest can claim neglect or insensitivity, then the minister or the government can be severely embarrassed and can be subjected to political pressure from the aggrieved group or interest. The potential for this type of political upset and pressure has been a factor in the minds of government members and officials, helping to keep them from neglecting any of the groups with which they have to deal.

Equality of representation among farmers?

Public policy concerning agriculture is to a large extent in the hands of organized, sectional interests. To what extent is this a democratic method of decision-making? In principle, there is no inconsistency between democracy and the type of corporatism we have been discussing. In terms of the model of democracy, particularly its assumption that decisions should be made by those whose legitimate interests are affected by them, corporatism may be seen as an attempt to hand decision-making over to the appropriate groups whose interests are affected. But are all legitimate interests equally represented?

116

The question of whether all interests are equally powerful is not one which admits of a clear and incontrovertible answer. Some unequivocal evidence can be provided, when direct pressure from a particular group produces a direct response from government, but these cases reveal only a part, and often the least typical part, of interest group influence. Much more influence is indirect, anticipated and even unconscious. Those who actually make the final decisions, ministers, government officials and interest group leaders, operate in a complex and intimate environment. Each will be conscious of the need to pursue the interests of those whom he or she represents. At the same time, each will be aware of the need to remain on good terms with representatives of the other groups and interests. In the continuing process of interest group negotiation, the groups who oppose each other on one issue may well have to fight together on another issue. Sheep farmers and dairy farmers may be in conflict about the extent of government intervention in marketing, but will be united in the desire to keep farm costs down. This process of continually shifting disputes and alliances requires an elaborate degree of give and take among the participants, a willingness to concede here and to gain there. Such tactical considerations will depend on the parties' priorities and their estimation of their own and their opponents' strength and what sanctions they each can mobilize. These factors will often be unexpressed by the participants and may not even be clearly formulated in their own minds. In such circumstances it is not possible to say with any confidence precisely who influenced whom and how much.

Quite apart from the difficulty of observing such indirect influences, there is the difficulty of assessing whether the influence exerted by various groups is proportionately equal to their numbers and the importance of their interest in particular questions. Again, some quantifiable factors may be identified, such as the levels of subscribing membership or the extent of representation on statutory boards or committees, but this gives only a superficial impression. What counts is whether such membership and representation are effective in producing equality of influence for those concerned. Moreover, the concept of proportionate equality is itself not unequivocal in application, and there is room for reasonable disagreement about how much a particular interest ought to be considered in relation to other interests.

Within these limitations, however, we may still assess the degree of equality of influence in the farming sector. Are all farmers equally represented or are some able to exercise disproportionate power? In terms of actual membership, that is the number of farmers who subscribe to their organization, participation rates are high. Federated Farmers claims a membership of about 85 per cent of those eligible to join. Most farmers, like the members of most other self-employed occupations, clearly see benefits in belonging to an organization which helps to keep them informed of recent developments and which represents their interests in dealing with other groups or with the government. The formal constitution of Federated Farmers is scrupulously democratic, a characteristic shared generally by interest groups. The business of the various sections of Federated Farmers is conducted either at meetings which all members are eligible to attend or by representatives chosen by open democratic procedures. The credibility of interest group leaders with government or other groups depends, in part, on their being able to claim that they are fully representative of the occupational group in question. Thus, as well as striving for as high as possible a proportion of subscribing members, a group must also be seen to let each member have an equal opportunity to participate in the organization and influence its policies.

Equality of opportunity is one thing; equality of influence is another. All farmers do not take an equally active part in the affairs of farmer organizations. Not everyone has the time or the wish to attend meetings or join committees. Effective participation in committees and office-holding at the various levels, particularly at the higher provincial and national levels, require personal skills in communication and administration which are not shared by all. Most farmers recognize that there is a loosely constituted class of 'farmer politicians', farmers who are particularly active in farmer organizations. In many instances, competition for office is not openly fierce, with many positions uncontested and nominations being made by incumbent officeholders. Advancement is thus more often by oligarchic co-option than by democratic competition. Such specialization in politics, which allows for an active few to participate to a greater extent than the rank and file is not necessarily undemocratic; equality of power does not require equality of participation. It is more important whether such specialization leads to rule by an élite, whether those who are especially active use their position to pursue their own interests rather than respond to the demands of the less active rank and file. Is there any evidence for supposing that the articulate actually override the interests of the diffident and inarticulate?

Those who are active in farming politics are more likely to be drawn from the wealthier and more established farmers, who have the education, time and local standing needed for successful advancement in farmer organizations. One might expect, therefore, that there would be occasions when the bias in the active membership of Federated Farmers would lead to a corresponding bias in the policies they pursue. An anonymous letter in *Straight Furrow*, expresses what may be a common feeling among farmers:

the rank and file members have no way of putting their ideas or grievances forward. If they go to a meeting to put some idea across they are overshadowed by articulate members often with political aspirations or an eye on a top job in the Federation. (*Straight Furrow* 25 January 1980)

However, there is little hard evidence of any serious gulf or real divergence of interest between the more and less articulate farmers. There may be farmers who deserve the name of 'farmer politician' and who come, on the whole, from the wealthier and more established farmers. They may even on occasion intimidate other farmers at meetings. But this dominance is not reflected in any serious neglect of the interests of the rank and file. On most issues which the various sections of Federated Farmers take up, there is little actual divergence of interest between the more wealthy and the less wealthy farmer. Such matters as transport costs, killing charges, exchange rates and so on affect all farmers; whatever the farmer leaders may press for as being in their own interests will also be in the interests of the rank and file.

It is important not to exaggerate the extent to which those who win positions of leadership in farmers' groups constitute a cohesive farming élite. The structure of Federated Farmers is designed to prevent this. Its regional emphasis ensures that influence stays in the hands of local farmers rather than devolving upon a small, central clique. Moreover, its combination of specialized sections and a general organization, each with its own officers, separately elected, draws a variety of different people with different interests into the organization as a whole. It is not that farmers are united on all questions — there are many issues on which there are real and important differences between different sections of the industry — but the structure of Federated Farmers helps to ensure that these interests are all articulated and where possible accommodated within the structure of the organization.

Bias is more common where there is a clash within the farming industry between those who are and those who are not full members of Federated Farmers. One such issue concerns the trend towards aggregation of farming land by farm amalgamation. Amalgamation makes economic sense, both for city investors and for those who own farms and can use their own property as security to buy adjoining farms and form larger, more economic farming units. On the other hand, such amalgamations help to keep the price of farming land high and to prevent new farmers from buying their own farms. This issue therefore divides the farming community and leads to a conflict between the haves and the have-nots. The clash was evident in the late 1970s when the National government introduced a Land Purchase Bill designed to curb the aggregation of farmland. The bill was supported by the representatives of young farmers hoping to get established in farming, that is the Young Farmers Clubs and sharemilkers, whose organizations are affiliated to Federated Farmers. The executive of Federated Farmers initially supported the proposal but subsequently reversed its decision, and the annual conference of the Federation in 1979 overwhelmingly rejected the bill by a majority of nine to one. In defence of Federated Farmers, one could claim that it was speaking for all its members, each of whom must already own farming property in order to qualify for membership. Certainly the clash in a case like this is less between wealthy and struggling farmers as between farm owners and would-be farm owners, such as share milkers and farm managers or farm workers. Moreover, the Federation did not attempt to hide the differences of opinion on the issue, and encouraged the share milkers to make separate representations to the select committee discussing the bill. None the less, Federated Farmers' claim to speak for all in the farming profession, full members as well as members of affiliated organizations, is dented by occasions such as this when it clearly prefers the interests of its full members.

There are others engaged in farming who may also suffer because their interests are not fully represented by Federated Farmers. For instance, those who engage in less traditional, or less traditionally respectable, types of farming, such as horticulture or fruitgrowing, tend to rely on their own independent associations, outside the Federated Farmers' structure. These associations are affiliated to Federated Farmers but their members are not full members. Given the size of Federated Farmers and the weight that it carries with government, there must be some additional advantages for those who come fully under its protection. It is not surprising, therefore, that in their dealings with government, horticulturalists and fruitgrowers, who are increasingly important to New Zealand's export trade, should complain that they get a less fair hearing than pastoral farmers.

In many respects, then, interest group activity within the farming sector is reasonably democratic. Because of the complex and flexible structure of farming organizations and because individual farmers are alert to their own interests, it seems that most farmers exercise a fair share of influence within the overall framework of interest group representation. Certainly, there are occasions when the interests of farm owners, particularly those in the more traditional types of farming, carry more weight than their numbers deserve. But there is little evidence that any exclusive élite within the farming industry dominates consistently in its own interests; there is considerable equality among farmers.

Interest groups and deregulation

Farming may be untypical because interest groups in this sector are more highly developed and their relations with government more intimate than in other sectors. Both governments and agricultural producers share a vital interest in farming, which has encouraged the development of an elaborate structure of consultation and co-operation. But if interest groups are particularly highly developed in the farming sector, the difference between this and other sectors is merely one of degree. In any major area of government activity, a similar network of interest groups will be found. The Department of Labour, for instance, deals regularly with the Employers Federation and the Council of Trade Unions, as well as with the many smaller associations and unions they represent. The Department of Health consults the different occupational groups such as the Medical Association, the Nurses Association, the Pharmaceutical Society, as well as bodies such as the Hospital Boards Association which represents hospital boards and area health boards. The Department of Education deals with the teacher organizations, and also with the University Students Association, the Secondary School Boards Association and so on. The pressures leading to the establishment of interest groups are the same in all areas of government: each side needs the other. Ministers and government officials need the co-operation and consent of those whose occupations and activities they seek to regulate or direct; conversely, those whose interests are intimately affected by government naturally seek to influence government in their favour as much as possible.

The interest group system has expanded rapidly over the last generation. The manifest success of those who are well organized has encouraged others to try to seek the same degree of influence with politicians and government departments. The steady increase in government activity, indicated, for instance, by the growing proportion of the economy taken up by public expenditure, has also increased the extent to which government impinges on the lives of its citizens and therefore their interest in influencing its actions. Improved communications, particularly air travel, have made national conferences and national executive meetings easier to organize. Interest groups have become an important adjunct to parliament as a means for the public to exercise influence over government. Indeed parliament has often been an adjunct to the groups, acting as an alternative supplementary forum of pressure for groups which consider themselves unsatisfactorily treated in the usual process of consultation.

Interest groups are clearly a vital part of democracy in New Zealand. For many citizens they provide an opportunity to influence the making of political decisions which directly affect their lives and livelihood. Since 1984, however, there has been a move away from the pattern of interest group consultation established under previous governments. In the months immediately after its election, the Lange government gave a strong commitment to consensus, attempting to forge new priorities through a number of national 'summit' meetings involving representatives of major sectors. However, the government soon adopted an economic policy which implied a lesser role for government in regulating the economy. Particular groups, companies, or regions were not to expect favourable treatment from government, but instead should aim to survive on their own. As the government and individual ministers adopted an attitude of economic 'neutrality', groups and interests, such as the farmers and manufacturers, which had traditionally been politically influential, found themselves much less involved in the formation of government policy. Even the trade union leaders, who could have reasonably expected to have had more influence under a Labour government, complained that they had less access to ministers than under previous National governments. There has also been a determined attempt to reduce the number of 'quangos', that is, statutory bodies and advisory committees, on the grounds that they are expensive and often unnecessary in a less regulatory political environment.

At the same time, the government created a number of state owned enterprises, such as the Electricity Corporation, Land Corporation, and Telecom Corporation, which are public corporations to administer public services that had previously been provided by government departments under direct ministerial control. On the surface, the establishment of new 'corporations' might seem an instance of further corporatist tendencies. However, the effect has been to lessen the influence of interest groups on public services. The boards of state owned enterprises are required to operate under strict commercial criteria and are free from direct government intervention. Thus individual groups and communities can no longer use political pressure to maintain services which are commercially uneconomic. For instance, a decision to close uneconomic post offices, for which local MPs would previously have been held responsible, is no longer a matter for government. The decision to continue or discontinue building dams for hydroelectricity, which had previously been subject to intense political pressure from the workers and communities involved, could now be made on purely economic criteria.

These changes may be meant to free the economy and society generally from what is seen as the dead hand of vested sectional interests. In some respects, however, they involve less an overall reduction in interest group influence as a change in the structure of such influence and a corresponding change in the type of groups wielding influence. In structure, there has been a shift away from the corporatist model, whereby groups and their representatives are publicly recognized as having a legitimate right to be involved in making decisions which affect them; there has been a corresponding trend towards *laissez-faire* pluralism, in which groups operate as wholly private organizations seeking to influence a government informally. As interest groups face a new environment, in which access to government and ministers is no longer constitutionally guaranteed, new channels of influence must be sought. To help meet this need, there has been rapid expansion of professional lobbyists, consultants who provide advice on how, when, and to whom particular organizations can press their demands. Such professional influence brokers are a highly developed part of the United States political system where the informal, open-market type of group influence is most highly developed.

As government policy is developed through informal rather than formal consultation, other types of interest have become more prominent. Most notable is the Business Roundtable, a group of about thirty chief executives of major New Zealand companies. In contrast to other business groups, such as the Employers Federation or the Manufacturers Association, membership is by invitation only. The group has become united behind a set of neo-liberal policies. They stress the value of the market, the need to limit the role of government in society, to reduce government expenditure, and to weaken the power of trade unions. Like most successful interest groups, the Business Roundtable, while claiming to aim for the welfare of everyone, is furthering the interests of its own members. Being self-selected from large companies, they have not needed to accommodate the interests of small businesses or of those in all parts of the country. Indeed, not even all large businesses have found the Roundtable's policies congenial. The opposition to tariff protection for manufactured goods precipitated in 1987 the resignation of the president of the Manufacturers Association, who was a member in his capacity as chief executive of a large manufacturing company.

The group's method of operation includes issuing detailed and well-researched policy statements, which it is hoped government will accept. In 1986, for instance, the group made a public submission on industrial relations in which it took a much harder anti-union line than the Employers Federation. Members of the Business Roundtable, individually and collectively, have ready access to ministers and government officials. A significant number of them have been appointed as chairmen or board members of the new state owned enterprises. They make use of seminars and discussions attended by leading policy makers and advisers and run by organizations such as Victoria University's Institute of Policy Studies. Again following a United States model, some leading members of the Business Roundtable have established their own policy centre or 'think tank', the New Zealand Centre for Independent Studies.

The independent influence of a group such as the Business Roundtable should not be exaggerated. Although much of their economic policy has been implemented, this cannot be attributed wholly or even largely to their personal influence. There were other equally important individuals such as the minister of finance and his supporters in cabinet, key officials in the Treasury, Reserve Bank, and elsewhere. Other important groups, such as Federated Farmers, have also become powerful advocates of the new policy of deregulation. None the less, the prominence of the Business Roundtable and its individual members does reflect a change in interest group dynamics resulting from a less regulated economic environment. To the extent that governments are less obliged to consult interest groups through statutory bodies and other formal channels there are greater opportunities for powerful groups and individuals to exercise informal influence directly on ministers and government officials. It remains to be seen how extensive and permanent the shift away from corporatist patterns of consultation will be. In many areas of public policy, formal consultation continues as before. Much government business and legislation, particularly of a non-controversial nature, is still effectively delegated to statutory bodies. In 1986, for instance, agricultural bodies such as the Apple and Pear Board and the Agricultural Pests Destruction Council initiated changes to their enabling legislation which were supported unanimously by both government and opposition. There are many other similar instances. In large areas of government policy, it is still quango business as usual.

Pervasive inequalities

The credibility of most interest groups depends on wide membership among the rank and file, and close harmony of views between national representatives and ordinary members; they therefore have a strong incentive to be well organized at a local as well as a national level. Though the interest group system provides important and widespread opportunities for popular influence on government, there are some significant respects in which this influence is unequally distributed in the community. In the first place, economic inequality breeds political inequality; the more wealthy the members of the group are, the more resources they can contribute to help their group pursue their interests. Interest group activity costs money. For instance, air travel and accommodation connected with national committee meetings or deputations to ministers are increasingly expensive. It is also desirable to maintain a permanent salaried staff, usually in Wellington, to provide support for the office-holders. Any organization generates paper-work and therefore needs secretarial assistance. The arguments which an organization can put to government will be strengthened by providing the right evidence; there is therefore considerable advantage in employing its own research staff to gather the appropriate information and present it in the most appealing way. Dissemination of information and arguments in an attractively presented form to influential people in government departments or parliament will also require expenditure on printing, postage and so on. Funds will also be needed if the services of a professional lobbying firm are to be retained. Quite clearly, the more money a group can make available, the better chance it can have of influencing government and public opinion in its direction.

In the farming sector, the interests of those who own farms, that is the more wealthy members of the farming industry as a whole, tend to dominate over the interests of sharemilkers, farm workers and so on. One reason is that the farmers are able to afford a much more elaborate and professionally staffed organization. In another area, the field of medicine and health care, the Medical Association, which represents doctors, is able to raise an annual subscription nearly twice that of the Nurses Association, which represents nurses. Its head office and permanent staff are similar in size and scope to those of the Nurses Association, though the latter has four times as many members. Admittedly, the importance of the amount of money spent on promotion and lobbying should not be exaggerated as a factor in the final determination of government policy. Some occupational groups with comparatively little collective wealth may have other sources of power.

For instance, employees in industries such as transport or energy, which have a pivotal role in the national economy, have been able to use the strike as a particularly powerful weapon in bargaining. There are also countervailing pressures from government departments which may have their own policy preferences, and from politicians who are sensitive to electoral consequences. It is not true that money is all, that government decisions favourable to a particular group can always be bought provided the price is right. Even so, wealth must be recognized as an important factor and the extent to which more wealthy groups are more effective in securing their own demands can rightly be criticized as a bias in the interest group system.

Just as important as the disparities between different occupational groups are those between occupational and other types of group. For instance, many people are not represented by any effective occupational group at all. People such as the elderly, the chronically ill or disabled, the unemployed, are not members of any recognized trade union or professional association which can speak up for them. The peak associations of employers and employees, the Employers Federation and the Council of Trade Unions, may look superficially representative of all sections of the community but they exclude those who are more or less permanently out of work — the chronically unemployed, the retired, school-leavers, women not registered as unemployed. Though the unions are genuinely concerned to reduce the level of unemployment, their major concern must inevitably be with their members, that is those who are currently, or recently have been, employed.

Where those who share a common interest are for some reason unable to act effectively on their own, they must rely to a large extent on others to protect their interests. They will find it difficult to generate the impetus and the bargaining power enjoyed by normal occupational groups. In terms of interest group politics, they become passive objects of welfare and charity rather than active participants in the processes of interest negotiation. Similarly, the many women who are not in paid employment outside the home are not represented to the same extent as people in the workforce proper. True, there are certain organizations which aim to speak for them. In the rural sector, there is the Women's Division of Federated Farmers which provides a forum for discussion of issues relating specifically to farmers' wives. At the national level there are organizations such as the National Council of Women and a number of advisory committees relating to specifically women's problems. These are now supplemented by the authority of a ministry of women's affairs. However, women are too dispersed and isolated from one another to act effectively as a sectional group. This is a general characteristic of many groups representing a general or consumers' interest.

In the health field, though members of other medical professions such as nurses may have difficulty in pursuing their interests in comparison with doctors, all groups employed in the health system can more effectively influence the conduct of the system than can the consumers, the patients for whom the system exists. The administration of hospitals can sometimes be criticized for being directed more towards the convenience of medical personnel than the comfort of their occupants. Though hospitals are nominally under the control of boards containing lay members elected by the public, effective control remains in professional rather than lay hands. It is, of course, appropriate that occupational groups should have more influence, person for person, than consumers or the general public. People's interest in their occupation looms larger than any single interest they may have as a consumer. On the other hand, the consumer interest, though small for each individual, is spread much more widely throughout the community and should on many issues be sufficient to outweigh the special interest of those more closely involved.

Attempts are often made to incorporate a public or consumer interest into the corporate structure of statutory bodies and other quasi-governmental groups. The membership may include representatives from local bodies through the New Zealand Local Government Association or nominees of the Consumers Institute representing the consumer interest. In particular sectors, such as health and education, there may be representation from the locally elected governing bodies, nominated by national associations such as the Hospital Boards Association or the Secondary School Boards Association. But it is doubtful whether such representation on its own is sufficient to guarantee sufficient attention for the public's interests. The lay associations are usually not as well organized or as united in purpose as their competing occupational groups. They are loose confederations of public bodies which are themselves made up of part-time, volunteer members of the public. They may represent great numbers of people: the New Zealand Local Government Association, for instance, represents all territorial local bodies and therefore all adult New Zealanders; the Secondary School Boards Association represents all parents and others who have an interest in state secondary schools. But if the interest is wide, it is also diffuse. Though all citizens have an interest in public health and the quality of education, it is not such a direct or immediate interest as that of the people whose work is wholly concerned with providing these services and whose livelihood depends entirely upon them. The charge of 'provider capture' made by critics of public monopolies may be exaggerated if it suggests that the consumers have no influence at all; but there is no doubt that the provider interest groups tend to have more influence than they should.

The occupational groups have a cohesion and unity of purpose which derives from the pressing interest of their members who will pay substantial personal subscriptions to their groups and, if pushed beyond a certain limit, may take militant strike action. The public associations, by contrast, are less well organized on a national level. While the Post-Primary Teachers Association maintains a large office in Wellington, employing over fifteen people, the Secondary School Boards Association makes do with one national secretary and a part-time clerical assistant. Moreover, because of the dilute nature of the interests of each individual member of the public in the questions discussed, bodies such as the Secondary School Boards Association or the New Zealand Local Government Association usually cannot claim with any confidence to represent the public, in the sense of being advocates of a consciously held or articulated public opinion. This must place them at a disadvantage in comparison with the occupational groups whose policies have often been actively discussed at local and national levels.

The comparative weakness of public or consumer interests, when they attempt to take the sectional interests on at their own game, can be illustrated by the history of CARP, the Campaign Against Rising Prices. This was formed in the late 1960s by a group of Wellington housewives protesting, initially, against a government decision to remove subsidies from bread, flour and butter. Its aims were to press for price control of essential domestic goods, particularly staple foods, and to scrutinize the activities of manufacturers with monopolies or near monopolies over the production of certain household goods such as soap powders and tinned foods. It attempted direct action by calling for boycotts of selected products. Though CARP claimed success for the boycotts — they certainly caused some temporary anxiety to the companies involved — there is no evidence that they actually led to any lessening in the rate of price increases. However, CARP did receive considerable publicity, which may well have helped to raise public awareness of rising prices and of the degree of monopoly control in groceries. The Labour party came to power in 1972 with a commitment to a policy of price control and a greater willingness than the previous government had shown to deal with CARP as a legitimate interest group. Thus, if CARP was successful in wielding influence, it did so indirectly through the parliamentary system, rather than as an interest group placing direct pressure on other groups or the government. It is the chance to exert political pressure through mobilizing public support which the politicians cannot afford to ignore which provides the consumer or public interest groups with their best hope of combatting the power of sectional groups based on occupational interests. Conversely, if the sectional interests can keep their dealings with governments and each other uncontroversial and out of the public eye, they have a much greater chance of influencing public policy in their own favour.

A further inequality arises from the difficulty which newly emerging interests face in getting themselves heard. For instance, when a new factory or a large public development is proposed for a particular locality, it will be supported by well-developed organizations with powerful resources and experienced staffs. Local residents, however, may have had little previous cause to fear any disruption to their lives and livelihood and will therefore have had no reason to organize themselves in advance. As well as the relative lack of resources faced by all small, amateur groups in comparison with large national enterprises, they have to face the additional disadvantage of mobilizing support for the first time. The same disadvantage can also occur among occupational groups, when new occupations do not achieve the same degree of influence as well-established occupations. A new group not only must organize itself, which takes time, but will also need to win acceptance from government and other competing groups jealously guarding their entrenched positions. Because of the time lag, the degree of pressure an emerging group is able to mount will always be less than is deserved by its current size, let alone its potential for expansion. Within the agricultural sector, for instance, rapidly-expanding new export industries, such as the kiwi-fruit growers, have had to fight hard for their share of attention from government. They have found the Federated Farmers structure, with its in-built bias towards the more traditional forms of farming, not the most helpful avenue of influence, and have preferred to deal directly with the government. There is a conservative bias in the interest group system, in favour of established groups representing steady long-term interests and against those set up to represent a newly emerging occupation or protect an interest newly placed under threat.

Certain types of interest thus tend to get less than their fair share of attention — those of the less well-off occupations, fragmented groups such as consumers, newly emerging or potential groups. An interest group system on its own is, therefore, unlikely to provide a sufficient degree of democratic equality. Though in principle compatible with the fair and equal representation of all interests, in practice it is unfairly weighted towards the more wealthy and traditionally powerful sections of society. This, however, is not a reason for discrediting the system as a whole; it provides important opportunities for democratic influence which could not readily be provided by other means. Given the growth of the government bureaucracy, a world-wide phenomenon, and the increasing number of quasi-governmental public bodies, members of different sections of the public should be encouraged to deal directly with these institutions in order to subject them to public scrutiny and to make them more accountable. It is unrealistic to see parliament as the sole means of public leverage on the activities of the government. But the bias in the process of interest group representation does mean that alternative channels have to be found for the more neglected interests to acquire their fair share of influence.

Countervailing 'political' power

Interests which are neglected by the process of group negotiation, can gain a hearing by having their case taken up by the politicians in the context of electoral competition. Consumers groups may be unable to exert pressure on particular producers or industries, but politicians know that each item in the household budget contributes to the cost of living and that rises in the cost of living are particularly damaging to the electoral prospects of governments. Again, ill-organized and fragmented groups, such as pensioners and housewives, may not carry much weight as interest groups, but they all have votes and their support is vigorously sought by politicians. The politicians will therefore try to ensure that their electoral policies are attractive to such voters, and governing parties will have a strong incentive to exert countervailing pressure against the sectional interest groups where the interests of such groups clash with those of other voters.

'Political' influence on the process of interest group negotiation is to be welcomed as a means of rectifying the imbalance of power in the community. The corporatist view that politicians should not interfere in the orderly process of interest group negotiation is, to a large extent, the self-serving ideology of those who stand to exercise more power if they can operate quietly, away from the glare of media publicity and public debate stimulated by party conflict. The 'meddling' of politicians, far from always introducing a distortion into the business of government, can provide a much needed equalizing influence. Again, as with the parliamentary system, we can see the misleading effects of an inappropriate political model. With interest groups, the inappropriate model, enshrined in the official structure of many statutory bodies, is corporatist, confining elected governments to the role of legitimizing interest groups and providing the framework within which they co-operate; interference from politicians, either through direct intervention or indirect pressure, is misunderstood as illegitimate and improper. Of course, not all such political interference is legitimate — any attempt by ministers to influence a decision in favour of members of their families or their friends is obviously illegitimate. Also to be deplored is the use of appointments to statutory bodies, many of which carry substantial emoluments, as patronage to secure or return personal favours. But interference on behalf of the public interest by a government spurred by a need to seek popularity with the electorate is not necessarily improper; it may be a perfectly legitimate exercise of democratic power.

The extent to which governments will be induced to intervene against sectional groups in favour of interests which might otherwise be neglected, depends on a number of factors in the parliamentary system. First, the government must be under scrutiny from all members of the public and must expect that people such as housewives, pensioners and the unemployed, are likely to exercise their votes to the same extent and as critically as other sections of the community. Political awareness and high turnout at elections are therefore vital; without them, there will be little incentive for governments to look beyond the powerful vested interests, and electoral politics will simply become a further extension of the interest group system. Secondly, a government must not be too dependent on the support of particular groups for its success at the polls. As we have seen, New Zealand political parties hoping to win a majority of seats feel obliged to appeal to all sections of the electorate, and cannot afford to be seen to be too closely aligned with certain special interests. Moreover, individual candidates depend on the party as a whole both for the policies they support and for the funds necessary for campaigning; they are thus less likely to become beholden to powerful special interests than if they were independent members, dependent on raising their own campaign funds and free to vote as they chose. Disciplined parties and party government promote rather than impede a democratic distribution of power.

It is no coincidence that the country where pressure from special interests is most marked and where the interest group model has been most vigorously attacked as undemocratic is the United States. In the United States, voting turnout is low, especially among underprivileged groups; party discipline is loose; and candidates must raise their own campaign funds, with the result that individual politicians are subject

131

to pressure from powerful sectional interests and single-issue groups. It is a mistake, however, to generalize from the American experience, and conclude that interest group activity is necessarily incompatible with democracy. The interest group model is not fatally flawed so much as inadequate, unless supplemented by a strong government which is responsive to the people as a whole. A combination of an interest group structure sensitive to a broad spectrum of sectional and local interests, and an electoral system which encourages governments to appeal to all types of interest, particularly the public interest, can provide a distribution of power which is in most important respects democratic.

This is not to suggest that New Zealand has reached a fully equal distribution of power. The parliamentary system does not treat all sections of the community equally. Those people and groups, such as Maori and Pacific Islanders, who can make less effective use of their right to vote are also disadvantaged in the interest group system, where they are more likely to belong to under-represented groups such as the unemployed or unskilled workers. It may also be doubted whether parliament and the politicians have exerted sufficient influence on behalf of the public interest on the steady growth of corporatism and the power of certain individual sectors. For instance, all New Zealanders have a common interest in seeing the export productivity of land expanded, where necessary by more intensive farming, including horticulture on rich land or forestry on poor. The representatives of the farming industry, however, are biased in favour of traditional, pastoral farming. Through Federated Farmers and the various bodies on which they are represented, as well as through close informal links with the National party, farmers have been able to impede attempts to restructure the farming industry in the interests of the public as a whole or of those who might wish to take up farming as a career. Similar points can be made about the disproportionate power of, say, doctors in the area of health or teachers in education.

Economic deregulation may appear to offer an alternative method of restricting the unequal influence of interest groups. Rather than looking to the government to represent the consumer interest and to equalize the influence of groups, neo-liberals place reliance on consumer choice directly exercised through a free market. As far as possible, decisions on economic production and on public services should be removed altogether from the government, where they are subject to undue influence from vested sectional interests, and made instead by the decisions of the free market. There is no doubt that in many areas of economic activity, the flexibility and responsiveness of the free market is a more efficient means of creating wealth and meeting consumer demand. It is doubtful, however, whether a reduction in government intervention will have politically less inequitable effects. The influence of sectional interests as such is not necessarily reduced; rather there is a change in the interests which are influential and the methods by which they exercise this influence. As we have seen, a more deregulated economy allows greater prominence for those powerful economic interests who benefit particularly from a reduction in government controls. The extent of government intervention is itself an inherently political issue, one where governments have the power to benefit some interests and harm others. A group such as the Business Roundtable, which is pressing for fewer 'political' controls in general, is actually seeking a political benefit for its members. The interests of the economically weaker sections of the community, which undoubtedly suffer under a regime of corporatist government intervention, are even more vulnerable if governments and elected politicians refuse on principle to intervene on their behalf. For this reason, a policy of extreme non-interventionism is unlikely to be politically acceptable in a reasonably democratic society where most people vote and expect governments to be responsive to their needs. Governments in New Zealand are likely to continue to be the main providers of social services and to be held generally responsible for the economic prosperity of individual citizens. Given the continuing importance of the public sector in New Zealand and the impact of government on everyone's lives, interest groups will remain an indispensable means of making government responsive to the citizen's wishes. The problem for the democrat is not so much how to diminish their power as how to equalize it.

FIVE: Local Government

The structure of local government

So far we have concentrated on democracy in central government, on the degree to which the central institutions of government are under the control of the average citizen through the parliamentary and interest group systems. But central government, though it may be the most important, is not the only branch of government. There are also the many local political institutions, such as city councils, county councils, harbour boards, catchment boards and so on, which come under the general heading of local government and which cannot be overlooked in any survey of the distribution of political power.

Under some theories of democracy, government at the local level should be the starting point of democracy, rather than being the almost forgotten appendix or afterthought which it so often is: if democracy is to do with self-government, the control of one's own life and environment, then the most important area of control is the most immediate environment, the locality in which one lives. Home and neighbourhood should take precedence over the wider and more remote units of region, state or nation, and the degree to which power is shared at the local level should be the crucial measure of democracy. The more decisions are left to be taken at the local level rather than by larger, centralized institutions, the more democratic the political system becomes. On this view, devolution and decentralization, movement from the centre to the local periphery, are democratic tendencies and their absence may be taken as evidence of political inequality. However, the degree of popular participation in local government in New Zealand and the nature of its relations with central government do not accord with a view of democracy which stresses autonomy at the local level. Whether this constitutes a weakness in democracy and whether centralization and concentration of decision-making at the centre are necessarily undemocratic can be considered after we have examined the nature of local government and the extent of popular participation in it.

The development of local government in New Zealand has been haphazard, marked by a readiness to set up new authorities and an equal reluctance to abolish any already established. History rather than coherent rational principle provides the key to understanding the overall pattern of local government at any particular time. The main political parties have been divided on the issue of local government organization and on how far reforms should be pursued against the wishes of local body members themselves. Labour governments have attempted significant structural changes even where they have provoked local opposition, while National governments have been unwilling to override local interests and have therefore tended to accept the status quo. In 1974 the Labour government, largely through the efforts of a crusading minister of local government, and a like-minded permanent head of the Department of Internal Affairs, brought in a Local Government Act which was an ambitious attempt to rationalize and co-ordinate the structure of local government. The case for reform was easily drowned by the protests of vested interests, particularly existing local bodies threatened with amalgamation or a diminution in their powers and status. The National party, when re-elected, repealed many of the more radical provisions of the Act. The Local Government Commission, the body empowered to implement many of the details of the reforms, was made more responsive to the interests of existing bodies. Some reforms, such as amalgamations and new regional councils, would still go ahead, but gradually and without serious disruption to existing local bodies. When it returned to power in 1984, the Labour government once again embarked on large-scale reorganization. The Local Government Commission was reconstituted with much stronger powers to override existing local body interests. A second term of office gave the party more time to consolidate its restructuring programme.

There are two main types of local government body. First, there are those most commonly associated with the term 'local government', the general-purpose bodies, that is, city councils, borough councils, county councils and districts. They are identified with a particular locality or territory for which they provide a number of important basic facilities, such as water, roads, refuse collection, libraries, parks and so on. The population of New Zealand is at present divided among about 230 such bodies, each with responsibilities for its own territory. Secondly, there are special-purpose or *ad hoc* bodies such as harbour boards, hospital boards, electric power boards, pest destruction (formerly rabbit) boards and so on. These bodies are set up to deal with one particular function within a certain area. The distinction between territorial and special-purpose bodies is far from neat or consistent. For instance, some functions, such as hospitals or ports, are universally performed by special-purpose rather than territorial bodies. But other functions, such as drainage or electric power, are in some areas performed by the local city, borough or county council, whereas in others they are under the control of distinct, *ad hoc* boards.

The last two decades have seen the emergence of a new category, the regional authority, with a number of specific functions, which falls somewhere between the multi-functional general-purpose territorial body and the single-function special-purpose body. The trail blazer has been the Auckland Regional Authority which embraces an area covered by a plethora of city, borough and county councils, and is responsible for a number of important functions such as passenger transport, drainage, water and regional planning. The rest of the country is now divided among a number of regional or united councils which at present have responsibility for regional planning and civil defence, but may be given further powers as part of a general reorganization of the functions of local government.

Within the territorial bodies themselves, there is provision for smaller, dependent bodies known as district community councils. These are small townships, large and distinct enough to have their own sense of community and common interest separate from that of the surrounding county, but not large enough to warrant a separate borough council. The Labour government's 1974 Act provided for urban community councils as suburban units within larger cities, but this provision was removed by the National government which preferred a voluntary, informal type of local organization within cities.

Local elections

In general, members of local bodies are elected by the citizens they serve. There are, however, some bodies whose members are not elected but are appointed by other local bodies. For instance, while the members of the Auckland Regional Authority and the Wellington Regional Council are elected, members of the other regional councils known as 'united' councils, are appointed by the constituent local bodies; so too are members of some of the less important special purpose boards, such as domain boards or museum boards. On the whole, however, local body members are elected and it is this which allows local bodies to claim a degree of constitutional independence from central government. It also allows them to contribute independently to the extent of democracy in the community. Significantly, proposals to increase the power and importance of regional government include the requirement that all regional authorities be directly elected rather than appointed.

In the case of central government, the election is the key democratic institution in the parliamentary system. It allows the people to choose their government; it also enables them to influence the decisions of government, either directly through the choice between election policies of different parties, or indirectly through the threatened sanction of electoral unpopularity. The democratic effectiveness of elections depends on a number of factors, such as a high level of turnout by eligible voters from all sections of the community and an awareness by politicians that their actions are being watched and will affect their chances of success at the next election. When assessed in terms of these criteria, local elections in New Zealand are much less effective than general elections.

The first, and most measurable, criterion, is the turnout of voters at elections. Eligibility to vote is now virtually the same for local as for national elections — over the age of eighteen together with at least three months' residence in the locality. Originally, voting was confined to ratepayers only but this restriction now applies only to a few special-purpose boards, such as land drainage boards and river boards, and to certain polls or referendums which may be held in connection with the raising of local body loans. The right of those owning property to vote in localities where they do not reside has recently been abolished and local body rolls have been combined with the parliamentary roll. Various methods of recording the votes may be used with the choice being left to individual local bodies. For instance, voting may be 'consecutive', that is spread over several days; or the ballot papers may be distributed and returned by post, a method preferred in many country areas where voters are widely dispersed. In urban areas, however, the overwhelming preference is still for the method used at general elections: attendance at local polling booths on a single day.

Average turnout varies for the different types of body. Voting is higher in the country, with turnout in counties averaging about two-thirds of those eligible to vote. In independent boroughs, turnout is usually between half and two-thirds and in major cities and suburban boroughs it is usually somewhere between 40 and 50 per cent. Higher levels of voting in the country may be the result of postal voting, which tends to increase turn-out; in 1986, for example, Christchurch City changed to postal voting and increased its turn-out from 36 per cent to 58 per cent. All these figures, but particularly those for urban areas,

137

are strikingly different from turnout at general elections which is regularly well over 80 per cent. They also contrast with generally acknowledged notions of civic duty. A revealing survey in one borough found that almost all (94 per cent) of those interviewed told the person interviewing them that they intended to vote in the forthcoming local election. Actual turnout in the same borough was less than half. Most people appear ashamed to admit that they do not or will not vote. They recognize a duty to vote at local elections though many consistently fail to perform it.

As might be expected, turnout is not only low but unrepresentative. Among those who do vote there is a preponderance of the better off and better educated. Those who qualify for the electoral roll through being ratepayers are more likely to vote than those who qualify merely through residence in the area. In larger cities, there is a markedly higher turnout in suburbs where property values are above average, and where there is a greater preponderance of people from higher socio-economic groups. Apathy at local elections, therefore, follows the same patterns found in other areas of political participation where not all groups participate equally.

Low levels of voter participation are paralleled by a lack of prospective candidates. Only in the major cities and suburban boroughs are there regularly more than two candidates for every council seat (the result of organized party activity which is largely confined to metropolitan urban areas). In other types of locality and for most special-purpose boards, there may be only a few more candidates than there are positions and, in many cases, there is no competition at all and therefore no need for an election. About half the mayors in New Zealand are returned unopposed and a considerable proportion of local bodies are uncontested, especially the less prominent special purpose boards such as pest destruction boards or land drainage boards where elections are the exception rather than the norm.

Where positions are contested and where voters do have a choice, the effect of the election is often reduced by the lack of policy commitments made by candidates. At a general election candidates stand as advocates of a detailed party programme, to which they are committed if they become members of the government. At local elections candidates are rarely so committed. Their election publicity usually consists of no more than a statement of their personal background and qualifications, together with some general and imprecise commitment to work for the good of the locality. Individual councillors will thus not usually be constrained by any specific commitments entered into at the election. One reason for the absence of detailed policy commitments is the comparative lack of party activity in local politics. The overwhelming number of local body members, over 90 per cent, list themselves as independent, without any formal party affiliation. Party affiliation is largely confined to the metropolitan areas, and is a product of the Labour party's policy of contesting local as well as national elections. Besides Labour, Values is the only other party to have ventured into local politics, with comparatively little success.

The presence of Labour tickets has provoked the emergence of anti-Labour groups, variously known as Citizens, Ratepayers or Progressive Associations. Labour party supporters claim that these associations are merely the National party in disguise, a claim which has some foundation: their membership often overlaps with that of National, and their interests tend to coincide with those supported by National. Yet the anti-Labour associations have no formal links with National or any other political party, and are careful to avoid appearing to behave like a formal, disciplined party. They do not offer the electorate a detailed election programme, but usually confine themselves to generalities. Their formal organization operates only at election times and fades into the background between elections. In this way, citizens' associations are able to appear in the paradoxical role of a party against party, provoked only by the activity of the Labour party in local affairs, without whose intrusion they would willingly disband and stand as independents. They can thus subscribe to, and benefit from, the widespread public belief that party politics have no place in local government.

Not surprisingly, Labour candidates almost always poll worse, on average, than their opponents. Part of the explanation must lie in the higher turnout from the higher socio-economic groups, and the relative apathy at local elections of those who vote Labour at general elections. Even so, one would still expect Labour to do better than it does in what is the heartland of its national support, the major metropolitan areas. Only rarely has Labour won a majority on a major city council. A further factor has been the use in most cities of the 'at-large' voting system in which voters choose from a single list of candidates drawn from any part of the city; this has often meant that almost all the successful candidates come from the more well-to-do suburbs. In 1985, the Labour government abolished at-large voting for cities with populations of over 70,000 which were made to introduce local divisions or 'wards'. As a result, Labour representation on the major city councils increased significantly. However, Labour voters are still reluctant supporters of party activity at local elections. They show a greater tendency to vote across party lines than do citizens' association supporters, and some Labour party members prefer to stand as independents at local elections. In Dunedin, in 1980, a sitting Labour councillor was disowned by the party for opposing party policy in his dealings with the city busdrivers' union. He stood as an independent and was re-elected, whereas another Labour councillor was endorsed and lost her seat. Such results provide a striking contrast with the defeat normally suffered by disowned candidates in general elections.

In general local bodies are not committed to specific election programmes. There have been some notable exceptions. In the early 1970s the Christchurch City Council was divided on party lines over whether a new inner city road should be routed through Hagley Park, and what new sports facilities were necessary for the forthcoming Commonwealth Games. The Labour councillors, then in opposition on the council, opposed the citizens' majority and fought the 1971 election on these issues. They were elected to power with a mandate to leave Hagley Park intact, and to build a stadium on a new site. Similarly, the 1986 election in Wellington was largely fought over the issue of the city's sewage scheme. Labour candidates opposed the scheme supported by the sitting mayor and council majority. When Labour won both the mayoralty and a majority on the council, the city was thereby committed to an alternative scheme. But such a mandate in local politics is rare. The general rule is for local bodies to have the freedom to decide matters 'on their merits'. If the previous election does not constrain local body members, neither does the next one. Local body members, being part-time and not depending on office for their livelihoods, have less to lose than MPs and therefore less incentive to work towards re-election. Moreover, they need not worry, on the whole, that their chances of re-election will be affected by the decisions they take or share in taking. Very few local body members are defeated in elections, and by far the most common causes of loss of office are death or retirement. Even where sitting candidates are defeated, the reason need not be connected directly or indirectly with their conduct in office, but may simply be due to the fact they have been opposed by better known or more popular candidates.

The 'stickability' of local body members, their tendency to retain office once they have won it, need not in itself be evidence of indifference to the views of the electors. In theory, it is equally compatible with extreme sensitivity to the wishes of the voters and successful anticipation of adverse electoral reactions at the next election. There is one area, at least, in which the electoral sanction does seem to be effective; this is the overall cost of local government. Income is mainly derived from some sort of property rating and all ratepayers, at least, are acutely aware of the level of rates levied. Indeed, because rates are usually levied and collected in one annual amount, many people will be more aware of how much they pay in rates than how much is deducted from their wages for income tax, though the latter may be much greater than the former. Unjustifiable increases in rates, which typically mean increases above the level of inflation, are generally unpopular and therefore avoided by most local bodies. As critics of local government sometimes complain, local bodies feel more strongly about how much they spend rather than what they spend it on. The urge to keep the rates down, or at least to keep increases in rates to a reasonable level, is reinforced by anticipated pressure from the voters. 'The ratepayers will never stand for it' is a common reaction of local councillors to suggestions involving additional expenditure. But beyond this general and imprecise injunction to economize, the voters *en masse* do not constrain or influence their representatives through the mechanism of the election.

The relative lack of party affiliation and of disciplined party voting on local bodies helps to lessen the accountability of local bodies to the voters. An individual office holder, like a mayor, may be made personally accountable because he or she may have to face an electoral opponent who can attack his or her involvement in unpopular policies. But where a policy is associated with a council consisting of a number of separate, independent members, it is much harder for the public to identify certain councillors as those responsible for that policy. There is usually no recognized opposition party ready to capitalize on unpopular decisions and to generate support for alternative candidates. Though there may be dissension within a council or board on particular issues, this dissension is unlikely to harden into the sort of permanent, public antagonisms which generate alternative electoral coalitions or parties. The patterns of dissension will be different for different issues with opponents on one issue becoming allies on another. A convention of corporate responsibility encourages decision by consensus, whereby initial disagreement leads eventually to a collective decision which all accept. Controversial matters are often taken in committee or privately and informally, in order to maintain an appearance of consensus within the body as a whole. By presenting a united front to the public, the individual members make their own positions more secure and lessen the public's chance of making them accountable at an election.

The lack of public knowledge and interest in the issues facing local government is reinforced by the media's neglect of local body politics in comparison with national politics. Television news and current affairs programmes are overwhelmingly national in their scope, producing programmes for a national network and therefore national in appeal; they provide a natural and effective arena for the political debate surrounding central government but not for local government. Regional television programmes, besides needing to entertain as well as inform, are still too general in scope. The country is divided into four television regions, each of which includes a considerable number of local bodies, both territorial and *ad hoc*; the usually very parochial activities of particular local bodies are unlikely to be of interest to the regional audience as a whole. Radio, particularly commercial radio, has closer links with local communities and can do a better job than television, but even local radio stations serve areas covered by several city, borough and county councils.

The larger metropolitan newspapers tend to concentrate on the activities of their main city council, though they may also attempt to cover other local bodies, sometimes through the device of special local editions for particular districts within their regions. The newspapers which provide the most thorough coverage of local government are those whose area of circulation coincides with one local body, or at most only a few bodies. This is the case with small provincial papers which often rely on the proceedings of local bodies for much of their copy. The growth of free suburban papers in the metropolitan areas has also improved the coverage of local government. But, even where media coverage is reasonably extensive, it is not usually controversial. It does not focus on the sort of conflict or disagreement which would help to associate particular local politicians with particular issues or points of view. The local media, in their coverage of local politics, tend to follow the same conventions as the local politicians themselves, preferring consensus to conflict, avoiding the appearance of partisan politics wherever possible.

In several respects, then, elections are thus much less democratically effective at the local than at the national level. The general style and tone of local politics diminish the importance of electoral competition. The competitive view of politics, which applies so well to national parliamentary politics, does not apply at all well to local body politics. Neither the expressed attitudes nor the actual behaviour of the participants, whether local body members themselves or the public they represent, give much support to the intrusion of competitive vote-seeking politics into local government. If we expect people to exercise the degree of power, direct and indirect, over their local people representatives by means of the electoral process that they do over national politicians, we will be disappointed. But this does not necessarily mean that the degree of democracy is less at the local than at the national level. The intimacy of local politics, the closeness between the electors and the elected, may provide other means by which the people may make their representatives responsive. Because the style and tone of local government is so different from that of parliament, we should perhaps consider local government in terms of a different theory or view of how representative bodies operate.

How representative are local bodies?

For analysing parliament, the model assumed that electoral competition between parties was the mainspring of democratic power. When dealing with local government, however, a more appropriate theory may be one that stresses consensus rather than conflict, and the independence of individual representatives rather than party affiliation. From this point of view, a democratically elected body is made up of individual representatives, each deliberating and deciding according to his or her own view of the public interest, unconstrained by pressure from the electorate or by factional alliances with or against other representatives. This is the official constitutional theory of parliament, though, as we saw, it does not accurately describe the actual democratic functioning of parliament and may mislead if taken too literally. At the local level, however, not only is it the official theory but it also, in many ways, gives the most adequate account of how local politics actually work. In assessing the degree of democracy in local government, we should examine the behaviour of local body members as independent representatives. To what extent do they act for the citizens they represent, or are they out of touch with the public, or acting only on behalf of certain sections of the public?

In the first place local body members are much better placed than their national counterparts to be in touch with the views and attitudes of their constituents. With the exception of some mayors of larger cities, they all work only part-time in their capacity as elected, local body members. For the rest, often most of their time, they live and work as ordinary members of the community. In this they are different from MPs who are full-time politicians, and whose hectic and untypical lifestyle inevitably separates them to a certain extent from their constituents. Local body members are in daily, routine contact with other members of the public; indeed they are members of the public themselves, as much as they are members of local government. Because they are so close to the community they serve, they will not wish to be associated with an obviously unpopular decision or policy, even

143

though they may not need to fear adverse reaction at the polls. Particularly in smaller, more intimate communities where many people know each other personally, the natural desire to remain on good terms with neighbours and acquaintances provides a strong motive for representatives to act popularly and avoid provoking opposition. Moreover, where there is a clearly articulated public opinion, many publicly elected representatives would accept a duty to take their lead from it. Sometimes, for instance, a strong and clear public attitude will have been provoked by a local body taking a decision which turns out to be unpopular. In Dunedin, in 1980, the city council accepted a recommendation to change the method of rubbish collection from rubbish tins to plastic or paper bags. This aroused strong opposition, particularly from those who regularly put hot ashes into their tins. Letters were written to the paper, a petition was circulated and a newly established local newspaper conducted a survey among its readers. In the end, the council gave way and allowed Dunedin citizens to keep their rubbish tins. The councillors certainly yielded to public pressure, though not necessarily out of concern about electoral consequences. More important was a general reluctance to defy a clear expression of public opinion.

But such cases are unusual. Usually there is no clearly articulated public opinion for representatives to follow. Local body decisions rarely provoke a widespread public reaction. There are few public opinion polls on local issues; letters and editorials in newspapers are not necessarily representative. In most cases local body members will tend to rely on their own assessment of what the public needs or wants.

Under the model of party competition, the degree to which parliamentary representatives are actually or typically representative of the public, that is, the degree to which parliament is a cross-section of the community, is relatively unimportant, so long as MPs have an incentive to compete for the votes of all sections of the community. But when MPs work on their own, out of the reach of media publicity and partisan conflict, such as in select committees or in the occasional free vote, judging issues 'on their merits', their own values and prejudices are much more influential. In local government, this independent, unobserved type of decision-making is the norm rather than the exception. It is, therefore, correspondingly more important that local body members should be typical of those they represent, that they should represent all sections of the community and not just the views of certain sections.

However, a disproportionate number of those who hold office in local government are male, over forty and of higher social status. The number of women in local politics has been increasing slowly, but is still a long way from equality with men. There are marked differences in the numbers of women on the different types of local body. The highest, or rather least low, proportion of women is found in city councils and suburban borough councils, where one-fifth of councillors are now women. The proportion of women in smaller boroughs is even less, and disappears almost to vanishing point (about 2 per cent nationally) in county councils. In special-purpose bodies, women are also almost non-existent. The one exception is hospital boards, where women have traditionally been thought able to make a contribution, but even there their numbers are far from proportionate to their share of the population. The lack of women on local bodies is not due to the expressed prejudice of the voters; there is no significant difference between the success rates of male and female candidates. The proportion of women candidates is highest in the metropolitan areas where lists of candidates are selected by local parties; those organizing a party 'ticket' feel obliged to appear representative by including women candidates. Conversely it is in the more rural areas, where the convention that candidates should stand as independents is most widely subscribed to, that women are least likely to appear as candidates. In addition, the social patterns of rural life, where women can still not easily work outside the home (or the home farm) and where travel to and from local body meetings is more expensive and time-consuming, work against the participation of women in local government.

Whether the absence of women leads to a corresponding bias in decisions is a question not yet adequately investigated. The traditional division of roles between men and women made women the best qualified spokesmen for the interests of children and family life. To the extent that this division is still maintained, the male bias in local government will have been prejudicial to these interests. On the other hand, many who support equality of representation for women do so on the ground that there are no essential differences between men and women; in this case, paradoxically, the lack of women in local government, though unjustifiable, would be of little consequence in terms of the type of decisions made. It would have no more effect than a disproportionate inequality in some other, quite insignificant characteristic such as height or colour of hair.

Another major respect in which local bodies are unrepresentative of the population as a whole is in the range of occupations and status groups from which their members are drawn. The disproportionate prominence of the higher social groups, which occurs among those who exercise the right to vote at local elections, is even more marked among those who actually become local body members. A detailed study of candidates in the 1974 elections showed that over half the candidates in cities and boroughs were drawn from what were defined as the first two socio-economic groups, whereas only 18 per cent of the population belonged to these groups. Well over half the local members population in urban areas come from the professions (such as lawyers, doctors and accountants) or from the management levels in business. In rural areas the dominant occupational group, not surprisingly, is farmers, that is farm owners. At the other end of the social scale, only five per cent of candidates were drawn from the bottom two socio-economic groups whereas 30 per cent of the population were in these groups. The dominance of the more wealthy was made more easy in cities by the 'at-large' system of voting. In Auckland, for example, most city councillors have usually been business and professional men from the more well-to-do eastern suburbs.

This bias in membership is reflected in decisions taken by councils. Because most local body decisions are made quietly and without partisan controversy, personal background and social connections are correspondingly more significant. Research into the influence of different interests and interest groups on urban councils has shown that the most influential are those, such as the Chamber of Commerce or the Manufacturers Association, which are closest to the interests of individual councillors. In most towns and cities, there are close links, both formal and informal, between local councils and the local businessmen's associations. On issues such as planning, public transport, or closing streets to traffic, councils will rarely, if ever, adopt a policy which is not supported fully by local businessmen and shopkeepers. In the country, the same applies to farming interests. Overlapping memberships between farmers organizations and rural local bodies, such as counties and pest destruction boards, ensure that the local bodies consistently serve the interests of farmers, even though farmers are by no means the only inhabitants or users of the countryside.

In the larger urban areas, attempts to involve more people and a better cross-section of people in local government have been made by setting up smaller, more localized bodies, to articulate and represent the interests of individual localities and suburbs. Pressure in this direction was most noticeable in the later 1960s and early 1970s, a time when there was renewed and widespread support for active political participation, particularly at the local or 'grass-roots' level. The Values party, then in its heyday, emphasized participation in its political programme, but the same concern became common among all those whether moderates or radicals, who aimed to make government more equal in its effect and less remote or aloof from the citizens, particularly the less advantaged citizens. Auckland city led the way by establishing fourteen community committees within the larger Auckland City Council area. The Labour government's 1974 reforms encouraged the creation of 'community councils', to provide a new, formal tier of local government, bridging the gap between city councils and citizens. The advent of new bodies with new powers threatened the position of existing local bodies. It was opposed by the Municipal Association, the interest group of the city and borough councils, and this provision of the Local Government Act was repealed by National in 1976. However, a number of local groups, under a variety of labels, such as community councils, neighbourhood committees, community committees, have continued to be active in the larger cities.

Opinion is divided about how successful these groups have been. City and borough councils, though they may informally recognize such groups as representative of local interests and have on occasion listened to their advice, have been reluctant to delegate any effective power to them. Issues which are highly local in character, that is confined to one particular suburb or section of a city, are relatively few in number and often of trivial importance, even to the local inhabitants. The attempt to involve the ordinary citizens, particularly those citizens in lower socio-economic groups who are under-represented on traditional local bodies, has not been very successful. On the whole, local committees are dominated by middle class, professional people, those who are already accustomed to attending meetings and joining committees. On the other hand, though middle class in social background, the grass-roots activists are by no means carbon copies of their local councillors. They tend to be more radical in political outlook and less oriented to the overriding goals of keeping the rates down and boosting local business. Unlike city councillors, they are more likely to support Labour than National, one of the reasons, perhaps, why the growth of community councils has been encouraged by Labour and discouraged by National. Though not accomplishing everything that was promised by their more enthusiastic supporters, community councils have, at the very least, allowed for the expression of alternative views and attitudes. On the whole, however, those actively involved in local government are clearly untypical of the community as a whole, a factor which must have an undemocratic effect if local government is seen as government by individual, independent representatives.

Another difficulty that local body representatives face is that without clear public support for what they do, they may have more difficulty in imposing their views on the expert, permanent staff employed by the local bodies. Officials, such as town or county clerks or engineers, are themselves equally members of the public, and may see no reason why the opinion of the elected members should be any better than theirs; indeed it will usually appear less valuable as it lacks the benefit of their experience and special training. Generalizations about the relation between elected members and permanent officials are difficult; the relationships are necessarily subtle and various, and little research has been done in this area. Both sides often chafe at the undue influence of the other, a sign at least that neither side clearly dominates. None the less, compared with central government, permanent officials are relatively more powerful at the local level. They are rarely subject to strong political pressure from the electorate. Unlike their central counterparts who are excluded from cabinet and its committees, they attend council and committee meetings. The scope of local government may be more restricted than that of central government and individual local officials may, in this respect, be less powerful than public servants in government departments. But within their respective areas, senior local officials are less controlled by elected representatives than senior public servants are by ministers.

Local polls

An avenue of participation which has long been associated with local government is the provision for a local poll or referendum. This is a form of direct decision-making by the citizens and potentially a highly important contribution to democracy at the local level. Local polls may be divided loosely into three general categories: organizational or constitutional, financial, and general.

Organizational or constitutional polls are concerned with the basic structure of government, particularly its scope and powers. Local government is legally the creature of parliament and central government can alter the legislation determining the structure and powers of local bodies without requiring a local poll. Local views are usually sought before legislation is introduced, but usually through the local bodies themselves, either directly or through their national interest group, the New Zealand Local Government Association. One area, however, in which local polls have traditionally played an important role is the reorganization of local body boundaries, particularly the amalgamation of existing territorial bodies.

Central bodies, such as the Local Government Commission, have consistently advocated a reduction in the number of territorial bodies through amalgamation. Until recently such schemes could be challenged by a poll of local residents. The failure rate of amalgamation proposals when submitted to local polls has been very high. There is resistance from smaller bodies, such as old-established boroughs, if they are threatened with being swallowed up in a larger unit such as the council of an adjoining city. Naturally enough, local mayors and councillors oppose the abolition of the offices they hold. Sentiment, history and community identity also play a part, but there are more immediate, material reasons as well. Amalgamation of a smaller body with a larger may lead to an increase in rates, to help pay for services provided by the larger body which have hitherto been enjoyed at little or no cost. It has not been difficult, therefore, to arouse opposition to amalgamation proposals sufficient to defeat them at a poll, particularly as turnout in amalgamation polls has tended to be low, following the pattern of turnout at local elections.

One feature of such polls, which is interesting from the point of view of democratic principle, is the disagreement over which group of citizens should vote on a question of amalgamation. Until 1974 the practice was to allow a separate poll among each of the bodies being amalgamated; if a majority of those who voted rejected the proposal, the scheme was defeated. In reaction to the low success rate of such proposals, the third Labour government changed the rules. The group to be polled was now not the members of the existing bodies taken separately but those of the proposed new body taken together. The intended result was to swamp the opposition of the smaller, recalcitrant bodies. At the same time, instead of a majority of those who voted being sufficient to reject a scheme, a majority of those on the roll was required; those who abstained were treated as supporting the proposed reorganization. Again, the effect was to load the dice in favour of acceptance. Subsequently, the National government restored separate polls for each of the existing bodies, but kept the provision that a majority of those on the roll rather than of those who voted should be required for the rejection of a scheme proposed by the Local Government Commission. The fourth Labour government in 1985 again restricted the veto power to a majority of those living in the combined area proposed by the Local Government Commission. (In 1988, however, it gave the Commission power to impose boundaries regardless of local opinion.)

Are all these different ways of conducting a poll on local body reorganization equally democratic or are some, as their opponents have argued, blatantly undemocratic? The question of which group is to be polled illustrates, in a clear and compelling form, the problem of deciding who the requisite 'people' are to decide an issue democratically. It can be argued that the residents of the smaller body are most closely affected, because it is their local body which will be abolished and their rates which may have to be increased. On the other hand, all the residents of the proposed larger body will themselves be affected in different ways by either an amalgamation or a continuation of the status quo. They, therefore, have a claim to a say in the decision. There is no simple answer. If we accept that all are affected to a certain extent but that the members of the smaller body have a larger stake in the outcome, then, in theory, the most equal solution would be to allow everyone a vote but to give extra weight to the votes of those in the smaller body. However, any precise figure put on such weighting would appear arbitrary and would be hard to justify. On the other hand, each of the simple solutions, allowing the decision to be made either by the larger or by the smaller group with each member counting equally, can be seen as unfair.

How large a majority should be in order to reject a proposal is also not a simple question. Particularly in matters concerning the constitution or basic structure of government which require widespread community support, the normal presumption is that changes need a substantial degree of approval before they can be introduced. A simple majority of those who bother to vote will often be considered insufficient and a more than simple majority, such as a two-thirds or three-quarters majority, may be required. What is more unusual is the requirement that a loaded majority is needed to reject a change rather than to approve one. In constitutional matters, the presumption is usually with the status quo: those who do not vote are assumed to be in favour of retaining things as they are. Strictly speaking, it is impossible to attribute any view to those who do not express one; in terms of democracy, treating those who do not vote as supporting a proposal is no more or less democratic than treating them as having opposed it. On the other hand, there may be less justification for requiring a loaded majority in order to retain the status quo than to change it.

Whatever the particular form of the poll, there can be little doubt that the basic principle underlying such polls, that the local 'people', whoever they are, should be consulted about the structure of their local government is an important element in a democratic society. Central government and its advisers may be convinced that certain units of local government are inefficient and should be amalgamated. This, however, should not give them the right to impose their views on the people concerned. The final judges should be the people primarily

150

affected, that is, the local people who bear the main cost of the supposed inefficiencies. Local government is not just a provider of services to the individual citizen. It is also, like central government, a creature and expression of community identity and citizenship and its members may put an independent value on their autonomy. As an analogy, we may consider the question whether New Zealand should be politically amalgamated with Australia. This is partly a matter of economic interest, but national identity is also involved. For this reason, the decision to seek amalgamation would need to be made by New Zealanders, not forced on them by powerful outside interests. Although local government is not legally autonomous in the same way as central government, the issues of local identity and community of interest are essentially the same. For better or worse, the ultimate decision in a democracy should rest with the citizens concerned.

The other types of local poll are less common. Financial polls include polls on local body proposals to raise loans on certain types of expenditure. Such polls may be held at the request of the Local Authorities Loans Board, a central government body, or by a petition signed by 5 per cent of electors. Until 1986, only ratepayers could vote in loan polls. This was based on the traditional, and no longer justifiable, assumption that only ratepayers and not other residents have a direct financial interest in the financial conduct of local government. Polls of this type are commonly threatened but rarely held.

Finally, councils occasionally decide to conduct referendums or questionnaires on matters of general policy. For instance, the Dunedin City Council held a referendum on fluoridation at the same time as the local election in 1959, in response to a vigorous local campaign opposing the council's policy of fluoridating the local water supply. Takapuna City Council conducted a questionnaire on the issue of social services. As with nationally-conducted referendums, this type of referendum is entirely at the discretion of the council; there is no formal or legal provision for the people to request one and councils tend to resist requests for them on the grounds that they involve unnecessary expense and are contrary to the normal conventions of representative government. On the other hand, provided that adequate turnout or coverage of the population is ensured, they are genuinely democratic in that they allow more people to have a say on a particular issue.

In general, however, the actual use of all categories of poll at the local level can hardly be said to constitute a major contribution to local democracy. Though local polls are historically a more accepted part of local than of central government, they are still used relatively infrequently and tend not to attract particularly high levels of voter interest.

Local and central government

The system of local government, though democratic in formal structure, is in many respects undemocratic in actual practice. The low-profile, non-partisan style of politics, the low turnout at elections, the lack of interest and controversy in the media, all contrast sharply with central government, and indicate a relative lack of popular power, both direct and indirect. Local body members are certainly closer to their constituents than MPs are, but this advantage is severely reduced because they do not represent all sections of the public equally and operate largely in a vacuum of public apathy. What are the reasons for this contrast? Why do the same citizens, who take a relatively active interest in central government and politics, show much less concern with local government and politics? Many reasons have been suggested, such as the absence of party conflict, the irresponsibility of the media, the inappropriateness of out-of-date territorial boundaries and divisions of responsibility. But many of these factors are as much symptoms as causes of local apathy. The fundamental explanation probably lies in the relative roles performed by local and central government.

Central government, though physically more remote than local government, has a much greater effect on our lives. Central government spends about ten times as much as local government. The power of central government to affect people's lives is greater and the stakes in controlling government decisions correspondingly higher. People will quite rightly give the central government credit or blame for public policies which affect them in many ways, such as general economic prosperity, health, education, welfare and so on. Many people are employed directly by the government or paid out of public funds. A change in central government can produce a noticeable effect on people's lives, in a way which a change of mayor or council will not.

Not only does local government spend less and do less, but those areas which it does control tend often to be less controversial and therefore less likely to stimulate public interest. Not that the functions performed by local government are unimportant. Many, such as roading, drainage, planning, water supply, are essential to modern civilized life, but they are like the act of breathing – essential but taken for granted and unnoticed unless they break down. However, they rarely do break down, and this contributes to the apathy which surrounds them. Moreover, local government is still subject to a variety of government controls. In many areas, such as public health, building codes, traffic control, the local bodies will need to follow regulations and standards laid down by central government and supervised by government officials. The ability to raise finance is tightly controlled. Loans need the permission of the Local Authorities Loans Board; any attempt to raise funds by new methods, such as a citizen's or resident's tax or sales tax, would require government permission and legislation. Where funds come directly from government, such as for education and hospitals, local control through hospital and education boards has withered almost to vanishing point. Similarly, much of the funding for major roadworks comes from central government and is under the control of the National Roads Board.

For territorial local bodies, the fact that such a large share of local revenue comes from rates on property and that local bodies are under pressure to keep rates down, or at least keep increases down as far as possible, helps to prevent them from taking on greater responsibilities. Any demand for substantial new expenditure, even in an area of primary concern to local bodies, such as public roading or public transport, will involve making submissions to central government. Thus developments which are out of the ordinary and likely to be controversial will tend to gravitate to the centre, leaving local bodies with the day-to-day administration of the humdrum and trivial. The same pressure from ratepayers has kept most councils reluctant to provide additional community services or to enter the field of social welfare, another instance of the unequal power exercised by those who pay substantial rates and of the lack of pressure on local government from those living in newer, less developed suburbs who are in greater need of welfare services.

Is the excessive parochialism of local bodies another factor? The great number of different bodies, both territorial and special purpose, together with the historical anomalies in many of their boundaries has been seen as contributing to the triviality of local government. Amalgamating existing bodies into fewer, larger units would, it is argued, create more efficient bodies with more power and thus generate a greater response and interest from the public. Similarly, regionalism, giving authority to regional authorities, each covering an area served by a number of territorial bodies, has been seen as a way of increasing local involvement in major decisions affecting a whole region. Such criticism of local body boundaries is widespread among experts on local government and has heavily influenced the reforms carried out under the third and fourth Labour governments. But it reveals a certain

153

desperation. Almost any other size of unit, it seems, than those existing at present – smaller, like community councils, or larger, like amalgamated city and county councils or regional authorities – will necessarily revitalize local government. But it is doubtful whether size or boundaries are in themselves very significant factors in the degree of public interest in local government. Much more important than size itself is the degree of autonomy. Community councils and united regional councils have both been emasculated by existing local authorities unwilling to surrender any more of what powers they have. Similarly, existing local authorities themselves attract a relatively low level of public involvement because of their relative lack of autonomy in relation to central government.

Centralization is a relative term and we should not exaggerate the degree of central control, by world standards, that is possible in a country as small as New Zealand. Much of the writing condemning centralization comes from much larger countries, such as the United States or Britain, in relation to which New Zealand is more like a medium-sized state or county or, in population, a major city. From this perspective, uniform control of hospitals or motorways for a population of little more than three million may not appear to be an instance of over-centralization. None the less, within the New Zealand context, there is a marked tendency for decision-making to be centralized. What are the reasons? Some cynics would look no further than the simple desire for power on the part of the politicians and public servants, coupled with the fact that, constitutionally, supreme authority lies with parliament and therefore with central government. 'Empire-building' is certainly a well-documented bureaucratic urge, and there are instances of centralization, such as transport in the 1960s and administration of electoral rolls in the 1970s, where the ambition of public servants seems to have been a major factor.

Centralization, however, would not have proceeded so far unless it were widely supported. Two factors seem to have been particularly important: economy and equality. Economic reasons usually centre on the economies of scale. There are advantages derived from the pooling of specialized resources, such as skilled manpower and expensive equipment, over a larger area and population. Small local bodies may thus become more efficient if they are merged into larger units. On the other hand, excessive centralization may lead to inefficiencies in the growth of large, insensitive bureaucracies and a widening of the gap between the providers and users of a service. Recent proposals for devolution of administration in health and education are inspired by such considerations. Equality is perhaps an even stronger centralizing

154

factor. New Zealanders have a strong commitment to providing equal facilities and opportunities for all sections and areas of the country and it is this, more than anything else, which has encouraged the central control of matters such as education, health, public housing, welfare benefits, broadcasting and so on. If local bodies had the power to raise and distribute funds for these purposes, different districts and regions would be treated differently, depending on how wealthy they were and on how high a priority their local bodies placed on the provision of particular services. At present, we are prepared to accept a certain degree of local variety in certain services, such as parks, libraries, or museums, but not in more important matters such as social welfare benefits, schooling, or public health care. Admittedly, New Zealand's egalitarianism is in part a myth, which may be used to mask existing social or economic inequalities. Even so, the pressure for uniform distribution of resources is a potent force in New Zealand politics, and helps to justify and encourage a high degree of central government control.

The important question is whether the high degree of centralization in New Zealand is consistent with democratic principle and practice. In theory, taking decisions centrally is compatible with democracy so long as the interests of each person in the community are affected by the decisions in question and provided that each person is allowed a proportionately equal influence over the decision. At first sight it might seem unjustifiable for people who live in Invercargill to have any influence over the size of a hospital to be built in Whangarei. However, if New Zealanders wish to maintain a roughly equal standard of health care throughout the country, it can be argued that everyone has a stake in decisions which affect overall distribution of resources for health; more expensive facilities in one place may not only offend people's sense of fairness but also the amount of resources left to be spent on themselves. On the other hand, complete centralization is unjustifiable. There are some decisions which cannot plausibly be said to affect the interests of those beyond a particular locality. Everyone may have a stake in ensuring that a new school is no better, or worse, than a generally attainable average. But where precisely it is to be sited, the details of its design, what colours it should be painted, how many pedestrian crossings there should be and where they should be placed, are hardly matters of national concern and should therefore be left to local discretion. Local government cannot be dispensed with altogether, but must remain as an important part of a democratic system.

However, if local government is confined to relatively uncontroversial and trivial matters, it will remain the object of general apathy and the preserve of the few unrepresentative citizens who take an active interest in it. In this respect, a high degree of centralization may have undemocratic effects, because it draws the life and interest out of local politics. There appears to be a clash between two types or aspects of equality, between political equality or democracy on the one hand, and socio-economic equality or equality in the distribution of social resources on the other. In order to revitalize local politics and increase local democracy, the scope and activity of local bodies would need to be increased but at the risk of causing greater variety in the quality of public services provided in different districts and regions.

This is the dilemma which faces attempts to devolve decision-making power from central to regional and local government. There may be economic gains to be made through transferring decisions from the centre to the particular locality. Bureaucracy may be reduced and time saved. Local providers may become more responsive to the needs of consumers. However, whether devolution will enhance political accountability and electoral control is more doubtful. Transferring a decision from central government means removing it from the oversight, however imperfect, of parliament and parliamentary politicians highly sensitive to public opinion, nationally and locally. Local or regional bodies will not attract the same degree of political involvement and generate the same degree of electoral sensitivity unless they have the same power to affect our lives as central government has now. If central government retains the main right to raise revenue for public services and to allocate funds, even if only in unspecified, block grants, it is unlikely that local authorities will become powerful channels of political accountability. The price of truly responsive local government would be a degree of local autonomy and variety which New Zealanders might not be prepared to accept.

Increasing the level of interest in local government might also be thought to bring costs as well as benefits in the heightening of political tension. If mayors and councillors were to become as embroiled in public controversy and political competition as cabinet ministers and MPs are, something valuable may be lost; there may be a positive value in the low-key, non-partisan nature of local politics. It may help, for instance, in maintaining a sense of community and co-operation between members of a particular locality. It has been argued that local government, because of its unaggressive nature, has an important 'integrative' function; it helps to establish a general acceptance of political institutions and a willingness to obey democratically elected authorities. Certainly, compared with ministers and other MPs, mayors and councillors tend to present a more consistently dignified and uncontentious face to the public. Their normal stance is that of official representatives who are spokesmen for common local interests or, where local interests diverge, are impartial arbiters between the various points of view of their constituents. They are also more widely respected and are less subject to the contempt frequently shown for MPs.

However, this apparent lack of partisanship is deceptive; it conceals the extent to which certain sections of the community, particularly property owners and private commercial interests, exercise disproportionate power in local government. The avoidance of partisan politics and the preference for consensus over conflict can operate like the powerful interest groups' disapproval of 'political interference' from politicians; it can be part of a self-serving ideology which supports the entrenched position of the more established and wealthy groups in society. Moreover, from the point of view of democracy, the influence of such attitudes and behaviour on the political system in general is far from wholly benign. As we have seen, the importance of political competition in enhancing popular control of elected governments is commonly misunderstood. Local government may be doing a general disservice to democracy, by fostering a misleading belief in the superiority of non-competitive over competitive politics.

SIX: How much democracy?

Recurrent inequalities

Having examined democracy in New Zealand in terms of the model outlined in chapter two, we can now bring some of the threads of the argument together and assess the extent to which political practice matches the ideal of complete equality assumed by the model. In many respects, there is a considerable degree of political equality. If we were making international comparisons, it would become clear that in matters such as voter turnout, frequency of elections, equity and equality in electoral distribution, popular responsiveness of politicians, the degree and diversity of interest group organization, New Zealand is closer to the democratic ideal than most other modern western societies with elected representative governments. But the focus of our argument is internal rather than international, concentrating on New Zealand alone, and here it is the inequalities rather than the equalities which are of particular interest. We will therefore summarize the main inequalities which have been identified and then take up the question of the political values involved in democracy, both the values which underlie a commitment to political equality and those which may be used to limit it.

In the course of our discussion of New Zealand political practice, certain inequalities have consistently recurred. One is an inequality of power between different sections or groups of the community. In many different respects, those who are in the higher socio-economic groups have been seen to wield more power than those in the lower. Superior wealth and education, particularly wealth, are also accompanied by superior political power. In the parliamentary system, for instance, those who do not vote – admittedly a relatively small proportion of the population – tend to be disproportionately drawn from unskilled occupational groups or the unemployed. In the administration of the electoral system itself, there are some slight, but significant, instances of discrimination. For instance, Maori who wish to vote on the Maori roll have been treated less fairly than their fellow citizens listed on the general roll. The National party, which tends to favour the interests of higher social groups, has had an advantage over Labour in the drawing up of constituency boundaries. Electoral inequalities, however, are relatively insignificant and the electoral system is, in general, equalizing in effect. The political discrepancies between rich and poor are much greater in relation to the other aspects of the political system. In terms of their numbers, the less well-off make much less effective use of interest groups; they are likely to have less ready access to their MP as an intermediary willing to act on their behalf with government agencies; in local government, they are less commonly found as members of local bodies and, by not exercising their right to vote in sufficient numbers, do not exert much direct or indirect pressure on these bodies.

The fact that wealth and political power are commonly found together is not difficult to explain. In many instances, particularly in relation to interest groups, financial resources are necessary in order to exert effective pressure on the government. Engaging in public life may require the ability to take time off from work which is easier for professional people such as businessmen and lawyers or for large-scale farmers. But in other cases the preponderant influence of the wealthy cannot be explained simply in terms of money buying power. For instance, the fact that the less well-off do not vote so regularly, particularly in local body elections, can hardly be due to any direct financial costs of voting. Other factors are at work, such as education, the degree of involvement and identity with the community and its institutions, the pressure of social conventions. These factors are connected with economic differences though the connection is by no means simple or straightforward. We need not accept the Marxist view that the economic sphere is all-important, that the distribution of political power is simply a reflection of the distribution of economic power, in order to recognize the obvious link between economic inequality and political inequality. Democrats wishing to increase the level of political equality may be able to make some headway through purely political reforms. But without much greater equality in the distribution of wealth and ownership, political reforms such as improved access to information or more widespread use of referendums, are unlikely to bring significant advances in political equality.

Besides the lower socio-economic groups, there are other, partly overlapping, groups which can claim to be less than fairly treated. Women, for instance, being less active than men in public life, in terms at least of being MPs or members of local bodies, are particularly disadvantaged in the less public and less partisan areas of decision-making in which elected officials rely more heavily on their own judgement and values. This disadvantage is compounded by the comparative absence of women in senior positions in the public service or in the permanent staff of local government. Similarly, the young, those who are no longer children but are old enough to vote and are eligible for office, are relatively unrepresented in politics. That they are not frequently elected to public office is perhaps not surprising, given their inevitable lack of experience. However, the fact that they also tend to exercise their right to vote less than their elders is less easily explained or justified and must have the effect of depriving them of their fair share of political influence. Again, the relative lack of participation by both women and the young may be at least partly traceable to parallel differences in the distribution of economic power.

Another possible area of inequality is in the balance of power between the general or common interest and sectional interests. Sectional interests, especially those of the more wealthy and longer established groups, exercise considerable power, particularly through the interest group system where they are consulted at all stages of government decision-making and may indeed take the initiative in pressing for advantageous policies or decisions from government responsibility for pressing the claims of the public interest when it clashes with sectional interests lies with the government itself. For instance, when the cost of living may be increased by higher prices set by producers or where public health or the environment are threatened by new industrial development, the government, in addition to providing a forum in which the special interests may be heard, will also need to be actively engaged as the advocate of the public interest. Attempts to incorporate separate, independent representation of the public interest into the processes of interest group negotiation have not been successful. Only government, with its control over public finance and legislation and its power to grant or withhold concessions and recognition, has the ability to curb the influence of powerful sectional interests. The politicians' desire for popularity with the electorate gives them an incentive to consider the wider interests of consumers and the public as a whole. The public interest may be dilute and without powerful, independent spokesmen, but it can be aggregated into an effective force through the ballot box. Certain general factors, particularly general economic factors, such as the cost of living, the rate of inflation, the level of taxation, the degree of unemployment, appear to be sufficiently influential with voters to convince the politicians, at least, that they must have regard for them in their dealings with sectional interests. The fact that voting turnout is relatively high and representative means that politicians must look beyond the rich or powerful for electoral support. Strict party discipline also enables individual MPs to resist pressure from special interests which may be particularly powerful in their constituencies.

However, countervailing pressure from government is not always sufficient to withstand the power of the major interest groups. Voters themselves are not motivated solely by the general interest. Individual members of the public are concerned not just with their own minute fraction of the public interest but also with their own sectional and regional interests which may also affect their attitude to government. Political parties seeking electoral popularity will therefore need to court special interests as well as public consumer interests. In the key area of industrial relations, a government may intervene effectively when the parties are in dispute but is relatively powerless if unions and employers make agreements on their own which are contrary to the general economic well-being of the country.

The weakness of governments acting on behalf of the public interest is not so much due to any lack of legal or physical power; it is rather a question of the values which determine what is politically acceptable or unacceptable. The growth of corporatist values, which accompanied the increasing power of organized interest groups, helped to obscure and disparage the role which an elected government should play in relation to sectional groups. The best government decisions would come from a process of negotiation and conciliation between the different sectional interests with which the politicians should not 'interfere'. More recently, neo-liberal theories have also discouraged government intervention, although for different reasons. Government intervention, it is claimed, will invariably lead to decisions biased in favour of vested sectional interests. The way to reduce the power of such interests is, therefore, to reduce the role of government in society; the public interest is best served by competition and entrepreneurial initiative unhampered by misguided government attempts to 'pick winners'. However, though there are undoubted economic benefits from freeing the market, it is not clear that an unrestrained market either necessarily reduces the power of sectional interests or invariably assists all members of the public. The power of some groups, such as the farmers and the unions, may be reduced, but others, such as financial interests and large businesses with international connections, become more powerful. Conversely, the position of the economically vulnerable is weakened still further and requires positive government support. So long as intervention from politicians acting under electoral pressure tends to be considered illegitimate, the public interest is unlikely to receive the attention it deserves.

161

Perhaps the most important respect in which political practice may not match the equality implied by the model is in the degree of independent power exercised by permanent officials, the members of public bureaucracies, both central and local. In earlier chapters we discussed various ways in which politicians or interest groups may influence government decisions and the extent to which this influence may be unequally distributed, with different individuals and groups being able to exert more than their fair share of power, through parliament, the interest group structure or the institutions of local government. The main focus has been on groups and individuals outside the government, such as farmers or the unemployed or property owners, and the comparison has been between the differing degrees of political power each group exercises. There is, however, another powerful political agent or collection of agents with whom these groups interact, namely the members of the government itself particularly the unelected members, public servants.

When discussing the parliamentary system, we saw that only a fraction of the decisions made in the name of the cabinet or individual ministers are actually made by them. The great bulk of government decisions are made by public servants under delegated authority. In some cases, the influence of politicians will be exercised indirectly, through politically sensitive public servants anticipating the likely reaction of ministers. In others, public servants will be expected to consult the various interest groups before acting and will therefore be under a certain amount of democratic influence from this quarter. But again, this will not apply to all decisions and there will be many instances where public servants will make decisions on their own without any significant outside influence. Similar inequalities also exist in local government. The official permanent staff of local bodies are also allowed a great deal of independent discretion by their elected superiors and by the communities they serve. This is particularly true of technically qualified staff, such as engineers, who have expert knowledge as well as administrative experience to rely on when dealing with laymen and the public. Indeed, because of the relatively low levels of political interest and electoral accountability in local government, local body officials may not need to defer as much to the authority of their elected masters. It is much more common for local officials, such as town clerks or city engineers or education board secretaries, to act as public spokesmen for their respective bodies or committees. Their national counterparts are more likely to insist that the minister defend their actions in public. In local government, the visible, public independence of permanent officials will make the task of supervision even harder for the elected local body members who are already handicapped by being part-time amateurs, lacking the time and the support staff necessary to master the details of their areas of responsibility.

How serious is the political inequality between public officials and the rest of the community? Certainly, there are many administrative decisions which officers of a department must take, matters concerning the day-to-day running of an office, such as who is to take holidays when or the colour of paper to be used for a government form, which are too trivial to be worried about. They cannot seriously be understood as affecting the interests of the public in any appreciable way and therefore need not be counted as decisions which should be equally controlled in a democracy. However, there are other, only slightly less trivial, decisions which do affect the public: whether offices are to open at times convenient to the public; whether a form is easily understood by those who must fill it in. Most such decisions are taken by the public servants alone, quite independently of any outside pressure. Ideally, the public service should operate within a code of conduct which puts the public first and encourages ideas and suggestions from members of the public. Many conscientious public servants are prepared to react positively to public criticism and will have often carefully anticipated it. However, in many cases, public servants, when criticized by members of the public, appear more anxious to rebut criticism and defend their own decisions, as if changing their mind as a result of public pressure were a sign of weakness rather than responsibility.

On more substantial matters of public policy, public servants are often responsible for the determination of policy as well as its administration. The major source of policy initiatives in New Zealand is not politicians, political parties, interest groups or other concerned members of the public, but government departments. That departments should use their collective experience and specialized skills to propose policy alternatives for public discussion is quite appropriate. But it is less defensible that they should have particular preferences which they hope to see implemented. As we have seen, many departments have certain long-term objectives, departmental policies which they hope to persuade ministers and political parties to take up and interest groups to press for. No doubt most public servants accept the final authority of parliament and ministers. But the ethos of public servants is not that they are literally the servants of the public in following and anticipating the wishes of the public wherever possible. It is, rather, that they hold responsibility for the conduct of government subject to limits imposed by the need to secure the approval, where necessary, of the minister or sometimes of cabinet and caucus and also to maintain

163

the general support and consent of the appropriate interest groups. That these limits are real and substantial has already been successfully demonstrated. But they leave room for considerable independence of action, particularly when reinforced by traditions of confidentiality and secrecy which surround government decision-making and are by no means sufficient to guarantee an equality of political power.

The intrinsic value of democracy

If power is unequally distributed in the ways we have suggested, does this matter? Is not a certain degree of political inequality desirable, even inevitable? This brings us to the final questions of value. A fully developed account of all the various arguments which can be advanced for and against democracy, understood as political equality, is beyond the scope of this book. It would require a detailed analysis of the main ethical theories, that is views of what the good life is and how it is to be discovered, together with the political consequences that may follow from these various views. We will simply summarize the main lines of argument which can be used to justify democracy and some of the counter-arguments which may set limits to it.

Arguments for democracy fall into two broad categories, which may be described as 'intrinsic' and 'instrumental'. Intrinsic arguments point to the intrinsic or inherent value to the individual of sharing in political decision-making, regardless of the results which may follow from such sharing or of the quality of the decisions which are thereby produced. Instrumental arguments, on the other hand, see democracy as an instrument or means towards other ends or values. They justify popular decision-making on the ground particularly of its political effects, in terms of the type of decisions and government which it leads to.

Intrinsic arguments in favour of democracy are typically based on some view of human nature, of what is the best life for human beings or of what all people are entitled to in terms of their humanity. One such argument depends on the principle of self-determination. Individual human beings, it is claimed, ought to be given freedom to determine their own lives; if someone else controls our lives, making our decisions for us, we have been deprived of a precious human good or of an essential aspect of our humanity. According to this principle, each individual should ideally be able to act for himself or herself without interference from others. This may work well for those aspects of our lives where no one else is directly involved in what we do. In many situations, however, neither communities nor individuals can act alone, completely independently of others, because what affects one will also affect others. Where there are matters which concern several people, a collective decision will be needed which is binding on all members of the group. Where a collective decision is to be made, the principle of self-determination may require that each member should share in making the decision. If everyone is allowed an equal say in the making of decisions which affect them, they are still free in the sense that they share in the control of their own lives. The decisions may not always be the ones they would prefer but, if they have shared in the process of making them, the decisions have not been imposed on them from without. In this way, a measure of freedom is preserved for each individual within a group so long as each individual is allowed an equal say in collective decision-making; people may not have as much control over their lives as they would if they were entirely independent of one another, but they certainly have more than if they had no say in making the decisions which affect them.

In our definition of democracy, democratic government, concerned with equal control of government, was deliberately separated from liberal government, concerned with minimizing the degree of government interference in people's lives. At the level of justification however, they may be connected, because both can be based on the principle of self-determination. This principle may be used to support the liberal belief that individuals should be left as free as possible from collective interference. It can also justify the democratic principle that where collective decisions are to be made, everyone should share equally in making them. This need not lead us to abandon the distinction; it is still important to keep the notions of liberal and popular government separate. But it does help to explain the strong connection between the two and why support for one is often accompanied by support for the other.

Another way of describing the value of democracy to individual human beings is in terms of human or natural rights. Democratic rights, for instance, are an important part of the United Nations Declaration of Human Rights. Human rights involve the claim that everyone is entitled to be treated in a particular way by virtue of his or her individual humanity. To deny people the right, say, to vote is to treat them as less than human beings or as less than full members of the community to which they belong. This would still be true even if a government which deprived its citizens of the right to vote provided them with a high level of material welfare and security. However well they were treated, they would still not be recognized as fully human. Basic human rights are all inherently valuable for their own sake and cannot be traded off against each other without sacrificing people's humanity and self-respect.

The inherent value of democracy may also be justified by connecting it with a particular pattern or ideal of human development. From this point of view, people who are politically active are living a fuller or more admirable type of life than those who are quite content to be passive and let others make decisions for them. This is another variety of the justification in terms of freedom and self-determination, that it is better for people to determine their own lives than to let others determine their lives for them. Both involve a view of human good, of how people ought to live, which requires that people choose for themselves and so develop full responsibility for their lives. To submit to someone else's authority is to fall short of the human ideal even if such submission is voluntary or the person in authority is recognized to be in certain respects wiser or more experienced. Dictatorship, however benevolent, stunts the human development of its citizens.

Some of these arguments, however, may place too high a value on political participation in relation to other areas of human life. There are other activities besides politics, such as family life, work, recreation and sports, reading books, watching television and so on, which may also be of intrinsic value. For many people such activities are more interesting and enjoyable than a high degree of political activity and, they might claim, are just as human and worthwhile. The equation of non-participation in politics with apathy is misleading if apathy is taken to mean general mental or psychological passivity. It is quite possible to abstain from political involvement without stagnating as a human being. That is, there are many other types of activity which can fully engage people's mental and physical energies. Political activity is only one such activity and there is no reason to claim that the politically inactive are generally inactive. It is therefore questionable whether political participation must be maximized in order for one's humanity to be developed to the highest degree. Indeed, a high level of political participation may deprive people of the time and opportunity to enjoy other equally human activities. This is not to deny the value of participation altogether. As we have seen, basic democratic rights may be possessed and exercised without the individual needing to spend more than a certain proportion of his or her time on political activity. But it is one thing to accept the value of a minimum degree of political participation for everyone as part of a rounded ideal of human development; it is quite another to insist that political participation be maximized, if necessary at the expense of other, non-political activities.

166

In our model, we attempted to accommodate this objection by not requiring a maximum of political activity from all and by allowing some to specialize in politics more than others. Though the model did not require equality of participation, it did assume equality of influence, with the less active people paying sufficiently close attention to the behaviour of the political specialists to ensure that the latter were responsive to their wishes. It has become clear, however, from our brief survey of the New Zealand political system, that this equality of influence is not achieved in practice. Many of those less active in politics are also less influential. They will often not know what the more active are doing; to be fully equal, the less active must at least be perceived as having the potential for forceful political action if their wishes are thwarted. Since differing levels of political influence are partly due to differences in wealth and in knowledge of how to organize politically, differences in political power could be reduced by greater equality in the distribution of wealth and in political education.

However, there may be more fundamental and intractable differences of value at work as well. Should we assume that all who exercise less than their fair share of power wish to be more influential but are somehow frustrated? There may be some people who do not take a particularly active interest in politics simply because there are other things they would rather do. If the price of their abstention from politics is exercising less political influence, it is a price they may be prepared to pay, at least up to a certain point. They may not abstain altogether and may take care to vote at elections and to resist major assaults on their interests. But within these limits they may be prepared to allow those who invest more time and effort in politics to gain certain political advantages. This is not to suggest that all political abstention or apathy leading to political inequality is to be taken as indicating contentment or voluntary abdication of influence: much will be accompanied by genuine frustration of political ambition. None the less, in a free, pluralist society where people are able to choose how to spend their margin of spare time and energy, it would be surprising if all chose to take a sufficiently equal interest in politics to guarantee equality of political influence with one another.

If other activities besides politics are recognized as worthwhile and if individuals are allowed to choose the degree to which they engage in political participation, a certain degree of political inequality within the community is inevitable. The attempt made by our model to reconcile equality of political power with varying degrees of political participation is unlikely to succeed in practice. Though theoretically possible, it will founder on the facts of human diversity and the variability of individual human preferences. While most would accept that the basic minimum of democratic rights are included in the ideal of a worthwhile human life, not so many will agree that their humanity requires a sufficient degree of political interest and activity to ensure complete democracy in the community. Political equality will conflict at a certain point with the rights of individuals to choose their own degree of political involvement.

Thus, though the value of individual freedom provides an argument in favour of democracy, it may also support an argument against democracy and in favour of a degree of political inequality, if such inequality is the result of individual free choice. Similarly, people may prefer a particular style of politics which works against the pursuit of political equality. As we have seen, particularly in relation to local government, there are many people who distrust political competition and controversy and prefer the low-key, non-aggressive politics particularly characteristic of local government. To increase political equality at the local level might require local government to be turned into a more contentious and combative struggle like national politics. This price might be too high for some. They may prefer harmony and decorum in government at the expense of a certain degree of political inequality. The intrinsic arguments for democracy thus support varying degrees of democracy depending on the extent to which political participation and the pursuit of political equality are seen as inherently worthwhile and on the extent of support for other, potentially conflicting, values, such as the independent worth of non-political activities or the right of free choice, including the right to choose to abstain from politics.

The benefits of democracy

The intrinsic arguments for democracy are, in many ways, the strongest and most fundamental, being grounded in basic notions of humanity and individual rights. But they can be supported and supplemented by a number of instrumental arguments, pointing to the valuable consequences which democracy may bring. One such argument, quite commonly advanced, is that democracy is necessary for political stability, that if significant numbers of people are excluded from their fair share of political power they will be disaffected from the regime that governs them and may seek to overthrow it. Avoidance of political upheaval and revolution, requires the active involvement of all in the political process. The concept of political stability is imprecise and needs further clarification: does it exclude only violent political upheavals, such as revolutions, or does it also rule out more peaceful, though radical, changes in political constitutions or regimes? The argument also depends on a factual claim about a link between democracy and stability which needs to be backed up by careful research. There may be some general weight in the argument at least as a defence of a general minimum of democratic rights. It must be admitted, however, that many clearly undemocratic regimes have remained secure and stable for considerable periods of time; the belief that autocratic and undemocratic governments cannot last and are inevitably bound to fail is over-optimistic and wishful thinking.

There are other instrumental arguments which claim that individuals derive personal benefit from democratic participation. By participating in the making of decisions which affect them, individuals will acquire a greater awareness of their own interests and the means by which they may be advanced. For instance, the experience of various community action programmes in the United States suggests that when members of depressed minorities become politically organized they also become more aware of their grievances and needs. Before they became organized they were not only unaware of how to achieve their needs for better housing, health and education; they were also unaware that these were their needs. Moreover, it has been argued, when people engage in political discussion and action with their fellow citizens they not only become more aware of their own needs but they also come to recognize the interests they share with each other; they thus become, generally, more community-minded. Unless, therefore, people engage in political participation, both their own personal self-interest and the common interest of society as a whole is frustrated.

How much weight is to be given to these arguments? We may begin with the claim that political participation increases awareness of one's own interests. This assumes that people can first be unaware of their interests or at least less aware of their interests. Is this possible? People's interests may be understood as what is beneficial or advantageous to them, general goods or goals, such as health or material prosperity. Can people be unaware of their interests in the sense of what is generally good for them or is the individual the best and final judge? At this point we reach what is probably an irreconcilable difference in political philosophy. Some critics of contemporary society, for instance, argue that capitalism has so distorted individual consciousness that most people are ignorant of their real interests, of what they would themselves prefer if they were free of the domination of a market economy. Similar claims can be made from the point of view of a religious faith which condemns the goals and values of others as misguided and contrary to their 'real' interests. Certainly, we must recognize the ideological influence of social and economic forces and that people's goals and ideals change with differing historical circumstances. Our view of our interests does not arise from nowhere and does not exist in a social vacuum. We are constantly under the influence of others and they of us. None the less, we must be wary of the paternalism, whether of the right or the left, which rather arrogantly assumes itself to be free of distorting influences and claims to know what is good for others or what they 'really' want better than they do themselves. Thus, though our views of what is good may be subject to change, each of us should be taken to be the final judge of what his or her interests are at any particular time.

On the other hand, if people always know their interests they may not always know what means are necessary to achieve them. They may know what they want but not how to get it. For example, they may want health for themselves and their families but may not know that immunization of their children against certain diseases will reduce the risk of serious illness. In other words, they may know their interests but not what particular action or policies are in their interests. Such ignorance is not uncommon in all sections of society though it may be particularly prevalent among groups, such as Pacific Islander immigrants, who are relatively unfamiliar with New Zealand language and institutions. Is increased political participation likely to reduce it? We may admit that involvement in political activity may be one useful means of increasing people's awareness of what is in their interests. Groups, such as farmers, who appear particularly knowledgeable about how to get what they want also have a highly developed political organization to represent their interests and participation in such organizations as Federated Farmers may help to maintain this high degree of awareness. However, as we have suggested, overt political participation, in the sense of attending meetings or serving on committees, is only one element in their success. Equally important are such factors as informal contact with other farmers, informed use of the media and general levels of education. Thus a certain degree of political involvement, broadly interpreted, may help individuals to develop a clearer understanding of how to achieve their general goals. But there is no need to increase political participation at the expense of all other less political but equally educative activities.

Similar considerations apply to the argument that political participation will foster an awareness of the needs of others and will therefore decrease selfishness and increase community spirit. By working closely with others, it is claimed, we may develop a sensitivity to their different needs and predilections; we may become more able and willing to sympathize and compromise. However, even if we were to grant that interaction with others generally increases a sense of community rather than antagonism, it would not follow that individuals must share in specifically political activity; the benefits could equally well be derived from other types of social activity. Arguments in favour of political participation commonly overlook, or reject, the pluralist nature of a modern society like New Zealand, the fact that individuals belong to a variety of different social groups, political and non-political. They tend to overstate the importance of politics and the advantages to individuals of participating in political activity, substantial though these advantages may be.

The most important set of instrumental arguments for democracy refers to the quality of the political outcomes which are produced. Democracy is valuable because it leads to better government or better political decisions than other forms of government. Within any community, it is held, the people as a whole are best able to decide any question that concerns them all and are likely to produce a sounder and more sensible decision than any individual member or section of the group. Such arguments often point to the 'common sense' of the average citizen or the superior 'collective wisdom' of a large group. They stress the valuable contribution which each person may make to a debate about a particular policy. Wide discussion and consultation before decisions are made will not simply help to reconcile people to whatever is decided but will actually improve the quality of the decision itself.

More commonly, this type of argument is linked to a particular conception of what counts as good government or good decisions, so that the connection between letting everyone help in decision-making and achieving good results is more direct and immediate. In particular the purpose of government may be seen as serving the wants or interests of all its citizens. The best collective decision, the decision which comes closest to meeting the interests of all the different individuals and groups within the community, will be the decision to which everyone has a chance to contribute. Leaving the decision to any other individual or group will not lead to decisions in the interests of all but is more likely, in fact, to lead to decisions in the special interests of those who make them. This argument will be seen to be closely parallel to the assumptions of our democratic model. Under the model everyone is to have an equal say in matters which affect their interests: or, more

171

strictly, in order to exclude those who take an unjustifiable interest in other people's business, everyone is to have an equal say in matters which affect their legitimate interests. That is, the notion that everyone should help decide what is in their interests, in the various groups to which they belong, is built into the model. So too is the view that the overriding purpose of government is to meet the expressed interests or wants of all citizens. This is the populist assumption which as we saw, is part of the dominant tradition of political leadership in New Zealand.

One objection to the view that everyone should help decide matters which affect them has already been suggested. Even if we accept that each person is the best judge of his or her interests, it does not follow that everyone is equally competent to decide the policies necessary to achieve them. Because modern industrial societies have produced and depend on specialized skills and sophisticated technical knowledge, individuals are not necessarily the best judges of how to get what they want. In any given field some are experts and the rest are not. In the area of health, for example, we are not all equally capable of judging whether a particular medicine is effective or safe and must take advice on trust from medical experts. Similarly, in the case of electricity generation we are not all equally knowledgeable about how hydro-electric dams are built or where they can be built but need to refer to engineers. In the economy, we may all want export receipts from farming products to be as great as possible, but only experienced exporters and traders will know where to sell what for how much. In education, most adults may be parents but they are not equally capable of understanding or evaluating the various methods by which children learn to read; this is a question for the educationalist. The list of possible examples is endless. In almost any area of our lives there is a body of specialist knowledge restricted to a more or less exclusive body of experts. The argument that everyone knows his or her interests but not necessarily how to achieve them supports a political system where the people at large set the general goals of government but details of policy are left to experts.

Even if it is granted that the specialist should offer advice only towards goals set by the public, it is not always clear where ends stop and means begin. In the example of building a hydro-electric dam, there are certain questions which are clearly technical, such as how deep the foundations should be or how thick a dam needs to be to hold a certain volume of water. Whether a dam should be built on that river or whether one needs to be built at all are less obviously technical questions. They may involve technical aspects, such as the likely demand

172

for electricity in the future, the likely cost of alternative schemes, but they also involve the setting of priorities between competing goals, such as the provision of electricity, the need for employment in the construction industry, the preservation of farming land, the protection of the environment. These are not questions on which hydro-electric engineers have any claim to special knowledge. They concern the balancing and reconciliation of the goals and interests of the different sections of the community, which should be the task of interest groups and politicians responsive to the various aims set by the ordinary citizen.

At this stage, however, another level of skill and experience has been added between the technical expert and the ordinary members of the public, that is the professional representatives of the various interests in the community, politicians, interest group leaders and so on. In relation to the highly specialized technical experts, such as engineers, lawyers or scientists, these people act as laymen, relying on their own general knowledge and judgement. In relation to the public, however, they may themselves be cast in the role of experts, skilled in assessing technical arguments and adjusting them to more general and often conflicting goals. The argument can then be advanced that the ordinary citizen, because he or she lacks the specialized political knowledge of the politician and other professional decision-makers, should defer to their skill, allowing them to proceed unimpeded with the business of government. The people may be able to judge whether policies have succeeded after a certain time and may register their judgement at an election. In the meantime, however, they should not interfere with those who have the responsibility to govern nor should politicians be concerned whether their particular policies meet with the immediate favour of the electorate.

Given the diversity and specialization of knowledge in a complex modern society, we may have to concede that it is simply not possible for everyone to have an equally valuable opinion on every specific political question which affects them. In a small and simple community, perhaps, where there are low levels of technical knowledge and everyone can know everyone else and share their experience, it may be possible for all to be equally competent on any matter which is to be decided. Indeed, it is often a desire for this degree of political equality which has led people to establish small communities or communes based on simple economic techniques and on social relationships which reject the specialization of modern society. This is a preference for social and political equality over material civilization and the technical and social differentiation which accompanies it. Again, as we saw in relation to the intrinsic arguments, there are priorities to be set and choices to be made. A commitment to increasing democracy at all costs would require, for most of us, a number of sacrifices which we would be unwilling to make.

However, accepting a certain degree of specialist and expert knowledge as the price of the material and cultural benefits which modern society affords by no means commits us to surrendering altogether to the rule of experts. We may concede that on many issues, particularly issues of technical detail, we do not have the time or the ability to reach reliable judgements and must rely on the advice of others who are more expert than ourselves. In private life, for instance, we often rely on the advice of our lawyer or doctor even if it seems contrary to what we would have decided on our own. However, we always reserve the right to reject advice or seek another expert opinion. The same should also apply in the political sphere. Technical knowledge must be directed to goals set by the ordinary citizen. The tendency of experts to overstep these limits and to encroach on the setting of goals is to be resisted. Engineers may be allowed to advise on how dams are built but not on whether they are built. Teachers may know how to teach but their view of what should be taught may be of no more value than their fellow citizens'. Moreover, much so-called technical knowledge is itself based on uncertain and contested evidence and assumptions and should be open to challenge from those outside the organized professions. It is one thing for the ordinary citizen to agree to refer certain matters to professionals and experts; it is another for these specialists to claim a monopoly of knowledge and to resist attempts by the citizen to hold them accountable or reject their advice.

Similarly, professional politicians and interest group leaders may perform useful services on the public's behalf but they should always be seen as agents, liable to be overridden or dismissed by their clients. Claims that the rank and file lack political experience or cannot evaluate detailed policy are to be treated with caution. Much of the criticism of the judgement of the ordinary citizen is, in fact, special pleading by professionals wanting to promote their own interests. For instance, it is often said that the electorate at large is interested only in immediate benefits and is not prepared to sacrifice short-term gain for long-term advantage. However, support for the long-term over the short-term or medium-term tends to come from those whose jobs are connected with long-term planning – bureaucrats, planners, academics and other experts who want their own views and projects to receive attention and whose income and security of employment shelter them from many of the more immediate anxieties faced by others. They naturally dislike governments to be deflected by consideration of electoral advantage.

They are therefore likely to support measures, such as an extension of the parliamentary term, which will allow more weight to be given to their own views of how the country should develop.

But whether the average citizen is so unconcerned about the long-term is open to question. Perhaps voters are not so easily deceived by blatant attempts to buy short-term popularity at the expense of tackling underlying problems. In 1975, for instance, National unseated Labour with a campaign claiming that the government was not facing up to the country's economic difficulties and that tough measures would be necessary. In 1981 National wooed the voters with a development plan based on a ten-year rather than a three-year span. In 1987, Labour sought and won a second term on the ground that the process of economic restructuring, though immediately painful to many voters, should be continued for the sake of long-term prosperity.

In general, then, we should remain sceptical of those who claim to know better than we do ourselves what is good for us or what will produce benefits for us. Certainly, we have admitted that individuals are not always the best judges of what is in their interest and that modern society requires a degree of specialist and expert knowledge. If we cannot share equally in making all the detailed political decisions which affect our interests, a certain degree of political inequality is inescapable. But this does not mean that no increase in the present level of democracy is possible within the general economic and social structure existing in modern New Zealand. For instance, more background information about government decisions which at present remains confidential, such as technical reports or economic evaluations, could be made available to interested members of the public. More people could take a more active interest in politics and keep a closer watch on politicians than at present, both at the national and the local level. Politicians and interest groups could exercise more effective control over the activities of public servants. Some degree of independent action must always be left to the specialists but the limits within which they operate could be much more tightly drawn and their degree of responsiveness to their various publics considerably increased.

Attempts to increase democracy, however, even if they are not incompatible with the existing social and economic structure, may again involve unwelcome infringement of other values, such as personal freedom. For instance, the major causes of political inequality are inequalities of wealth and education. If these inequalities were to be significantly reduced, the personal freedom of individuals and their families might have to be restricted. For example, the freedom to bequeath property to one's children, one of the main causes of economic

175

inequality, would need to be curtailed. So too would the right to purchase superior education, through private schools or through buying a house in an area served by a better school. Such measures would be seen by some people as intolerable invasions of personal liberty. Similar liberal objections could be made against attempts to foster a higher general level of interest in politics and government decisions. Even a minor change, such as showing more political programmes in prime time on television, would for many people be an unacceptable intrusion into their leisure. This is not to say that the status quo represents a perfect balance or that we should be content with the degree of political equality so far achieved; there are certainly many areas in which improvements could be made without any substantial loss of other values. We must recognize, however, that the search for democracy may bring us into conflict with other values, such as material comfort or personal freedom. Where the balance is to be struck between these competing values is a matter for individual judgement and a question on which reasonable people may disagree. However, any society which claims to be tolerably democratic should at least provide that the degree of weight to be given to political equality in relation to other personal and social goods has the broad support of the community as a whole. Whether this is true of the distribution of political power in New Zealand must remain an open question.

Bibliographical notes

Chapter One

P.11 *'Democracy'*. The modern academic literature on democracy is vast and can only be briefly touched on in these notes. A good all-round introduction is Jack Lively *Democracy* (Oxford, 1975). Carl Cohen *Democracy* (Athens, Georgia, 1971) concentrates on the more philosophical issues. David Held *Models of Democracy* (Cambridge, Oxford, 1987) gives a historical account of different models of democracy. Barry Holden *The Nature of Democracy* (London, 1974) and J. Roland Pennock *Democratic Political Theory* (Princeton, 1979) have full bibliographical notes. Lincoln's famous triad in the Gettysburg Address is not actually linked to the word 'democracy'.

P. 16 *The minimum conception of democracy*. Schumpeter's definition (see page 9) is the most influential of modern, minimum definitions. Criticism of minimum definitions as ideologically conservative is found in Graeme Duncan and Steven Lukes 'The new democracy' *Political Studies* 11 (1963) 156-77; Peter Bachrach *The Theory of Democratic Elitism* (Boston and Toronto, 1967).

P.21 *Democracy and liberalism*. For the tension between the democratic principle of political equality and the liberal principle of limited government, see David Miller 'Democracy and social justice' in Pierre Birnbaum, Jack Lively and Geraint Parry (eds) *Democracy, Consensus and Social Contract* (London and Beverly Hills, 1978) 75-100.

P.25 *Pluralism*. The pluralist theory of democracy is especially associated with Robert A. Dahl and his concept of 'polyarchy', a type of democratic government in which power is dispersed among a plurality of groups. See Robert A. Dahl *A Preface to Democratic Theory* (Chicago, 1956); *After the Revolution?* (New Haven and London, 1970); *Polyarchy* (New Haven and London, 1971); *Dilemmas of Pluralist Democracy* (New Haven and London 1982). *A Preface to Democratic Theory*, Ch. 4, contains the classic discussion of democratic intensity. See also R. G. Mulgan 'Who should have how much say about what?' *Political Science* 36 (1984) 112-24. In *After The Revolution?*, Ch. 2, Dahl discusses the problem, commonly neglected, of who should count as 'the people' for any particular issue. See also Robert A. Dahl 'Procedural democracy' in Peter Laslett and J. Fishkin (ed) *Philosophy, Politics and Society*, 5th Series (Oxford, 1979) 167-92.

P.25 *Interests*. For differing views of interests see Brian Barry *Political Argument* (London, 1965) Ch. 10; William E. Connolly, *The Terms of Political Discourse* (Lexington, 1974) Ch. 2; Christine Swanton 'The concept of interests' *Political Theory* 8 (1980) 83-101.

P.29 *Power.* A good introduction to the analytical problems associated with the concept of political power is Steven Lukes *Power: A Radical View* (London, 1974), though Lukes' own solution, that power is affecting people contrary to their interests, is not followed here.

P.32 *'Anticipated reactions'.* Their importance in modern democracy is stressed by Giovanni Sartori in *Democratic Theory* (Detroit, 1962) and *The Theory of Democracy Revisited* (Chatham, 1987) Ch. 6.

Chapter Two

P.41 *Pluralism and the public interest.* Certain influential American pluralists such as David B. Truman *The Governmental Process* (New York, 1951) and Robert A. Dahl *Who Governs?* (New Haven, 1961), have tended to view the political process as purely a bargaining process between sectional interests. For the criticism that they overlook the public or community interest see, for example, E. E. Schattschneider *The Semisovereign People* (New York, 1960) Ch. 2; Theodore J. Lowi *The End of Liberalism* 2nd edition (New York and London 1979) Chs 2-3; L. J. Sharpe 'American democracy reconsidered' *British Journal of Political Science* 3 (1973) 144-8; William A. Kelso *American Democratic Theory* (Westport and London, 1978) Chs 2, 5, 6.

P.43 *Apathy.* For criticism of the argument that pluralism equates political apathy with political satisfaction, see Jack L. Walker 'A critique of the elitist theory of democracy' *American Political Science Review* 60 (1966) 285-295.

P.44 *Self-interest and participation.* For the argument that self-interest is not sufficient to guarantee participation by an egoist, see Mancur Olson *The Logic of Collective Action* (Cambridge, 1965); Brian M. Barry *Sociologists, Economists and Democracy* (London, 1970) Ch. 2; R. Hardin *Collective Action* (Baltimore, 1982).

P.45 *Political development in New Zealand.* For the development of political institutions in New Zealand, see W. H. Oliver with B. R. Williams (ed) *The Oxford History of New Zealand* (Oxford and Wellington, 1981) Chs 4, 8, 13. For criticism of the suggested model as too dependent on actual New Zealand politics, see the review of the first edition of this book by E. M. McLeay *Political Science* 36 (1984) 174-8.

P.49 *Pragmatism.* The pragmatism of New Zealand politicians was criticized by Keith Ovenden 'On the absence of political ideas' in Ray Goldstein with Rod Alley (ed) *Labour in Power–Promise and Performance* (Wellington, 1975) 190-7.

P.50 For Maori politics and methods of decision-making, see J. Metge, *The Maoris of New Zealand* (London, 1976) Chs 14-15; J. McRae 'The function and style of Ruunanga in Maori politics' *Journal of the Polynesian Society* 93 (1984) 283-94; S. Levine and R. Vasil *Maori Political Perspectives* (Auckland, 1985). See also G. A. Wood 'Race and politics in New Zealand' in Stephen Levine (ed) *Politics in New Zealand* (Sydney, 1978) 334-42; Richard Mulgan 'Aotearoa – New Zealand? Problems of bicultural democracy' in *Government in the 1990s* (Dunedin, 1988) 26-42.

Chapter Three

P.56 *New Zealand politics.* Useful general introductions to New Zealand politics are Keith Jackson *New Zealand: Politics of Change* (Wellington, 1973); Stephen Levine *The New Zealand Political System* (Sydney, 1979); Les Cleveland *The Politics of Utopia* (Wellington, 1979); G. A. Wood *Governing New Zealand* (Auckland, forthcoming 1988). Austin Mitchell *Politics and People in New Zealand* (Christchurch, 1969) contains essays on New Zealand politics. H. Gold (ed) *New Zealand Politics in Perspective* (Auckland, 1985) contains articles on most of the main aspects of New Zealand government.

P.56 *Parliament.* For a view of parliament's functions which places less emphasis on political parties and more on the division between executive and legislature, see Geoffrey Palmer *Unbridled Power* (Auckland, 1987). For explicit criticism of the author's view of parliament, see Keith Jackson *The Dilemma of Parliament* (Wellington, 1987), esp. xi-xii. See also *Report of the Royal Commission on the Electoral System 'Towards a Better Democracy'* (Wellington, 1986) Ch. 4.

P.57 *Political parties.* For the history of political parties in New Zealand, see R. S. Milne *Political Parties in New Zealand* (Oxford, 1966). For up-to-date introductions to the main parties, see Howard R. Penniman (ed) *New Zealand at the Polls* (Washington, 1980), Chs 5-7. H. Gold (ed) *New Zealand Politics in Perspective* (Auckland, 1985) Chs 14-18.

P.58 *Caucus.* For assessments of the importance of caucus in the New Zealand parliament, see Austin Mitchell 'Caucus: the New Zealand parliamentary parties' *Journal of Commonwealth Political Studies* 6 (1968) 3-33; Keith Jackson 'Caucus: the anti-parliament system?' *Parliamentarian* 59 (1978) 159-64; Roderic M. Alley 'Parliamentary parties in office: government-backbench relations' in Stephen Levine (ed) *Politics in New Zealand* (Sydney, 1978) 96-114; Keith Jackson *The Dilemma of Parliament* (Wellington, 1987) Ch. 5.

P.59 *Party competition.* The assumption that political parties compete for the voters' support in a way analagous to companies aiming to maximize sales in a competitive market was developed by Anthony Downs *An Economic Theory of Democracy* (New York, 1957).

P.63 *Mandate.* For the importance of the electoral mandate in New Zealand, see R. G. Mulgan 'The concept of mandate in New Zealand politics', *Political Science* 30 (1978) 88-96. The use made of the election policy by Kirk and Muldoon is documented respectively in Tony Garnier, Bruce Kohn and Pat Booth *The Hunter and the Hill* (Auckland, 1978) 90-2 and 'Inside the government machine' edited version of an interview by Austin Mitchell *New Zealand Listener* (15 December 1979) 62. See also Roderic M. Alley 'Parliamentary parties in office: government-backbench relations' in Stephen Levine (ed) *Politics in New Zealand* (Sydney, 1978) 104; Marilyn Waring in J. Stephen Hoadley (ed) *Improving New Zealand's Democracy* (Auckland, 1979) 56.

P.71 *Voter rationality.* Useful general discussions of voter rationality and of whether voting research has proved that voters are irrational may be found in J. P. Plamenatz 'Electoral studies and democratic theory' *Political Studies* 6(1958) 1-9; Brian Barry *Sociologists, Economists and Democracy* (London, 1970), Chs 2, 5, 6; Dennis F. Thompson *The Democratic Citizen* (Cambridge, 1970). Whether or not the decisions of New Zealand voters are affected by primarily economic conditions is a matter of dispute; see Paul A. Gough and

Gregory G. Brunk 'Are economic conditions really important for New Zealand elections?' *Political Science* 33 (1981) 1-9. See also H. Gold 'The social bias of party choice' in H. Gold (ed) *New Zealand Politics in Perspective* (Auckland, 1985) 320-33; James W. Lamare 'Party identification and voting behaviour in New Zealand' *Political Science* 36 (1984) 1-9; Jack Vowles 'Social structure and political attitudes: a report of 1984 election voting in three Auckland marginals' *Political Science* 39 (1987) 17-31.

P.74 *Term of parliament.* See *Report of the Royal Commission on the Electoral System 'Towards a Better Democracy'* (Wellington, 1986) Ch. 6.

P.75 *Politicians and public servants.* For the responsiveness of public servants to the electoral policy of a new government, see Keith Jackson 'Government succession in New Zealand' in Stephen Levine (ed) *Politics in New Zealand* (Sydney, 1978) 1-23. For departmental policy, see Lloyd White 'Policy and politicians' *New Zealand International Review* 4, 2(1979) 16-17; Aynsley J. Kellow 'Politicians versus bureaucrats: who makes public policy?' in H. Gold (ed) *New Zealand Politics in Perspective* (Auckland, 1985) 104-11; John Roberts, *Politicians, Public Servants and Public Enterprise* (Wellington, 1987). For the survey of middle-ranking public servants see Thomas B. Smith *The New Zealand Bureaucrat* (Wellington, 1974) esp. Ch. 11; see also Keith Jackson 'Cabinet and prime minister' in Stephen Levine (ed) *Politics in New Zealand* (Sydney, 1978) 63-77; R. M. Alley (ed) *State Servants and the Public in the 1980s* (Wellington, 1980).

P.78 *Voting in New Zealand.* For patterns of support for the different parties see R. M. Chapman 'From Labour to National' in W. H. Oliver with B. R. Williams (ed) *The Oxford History of New Zealand* (Oxford and Wellington, 1981) Ch. 13; Austin Mitchell *Politics and People in New Zealand* (Christchurch, 1969) 203-228; R. H. Brookes 'Representative government and the elector' *New Zealand Journal of Public Administration* 33, 2 (1971) 1-19. The electoral system and its administration are described by Alan McRobie in Howard R. Penniman (ed) *New Zealand at the Polls* (Wellington, 1980) 64-98. See also *Report of the Royal Commission on the Electoral System 'Towards a Better Democracy'* (Wellington, 1986).

P.81 *Maori Representation.* For the organization of Maori electorates see Alan D. McRobie 'Ethnic representation: the New Zealand experience' ibid. 270-283; *Report of the Royal Commission on the Electoral System 'Towards a Better Democracy'* (Wellington, 1986) Ch. 3 and Appendix B (A history of Maori representation in parliament by M. P. K. Sorrenson).

P.89 *Proportional representation.* General accounts of alternative electoral systems may be found in Enid Lakeman *How Democracies Vote* 4th edition (London, 1974); Douglas W. Rae *The Political Consequences of Electoral Laws* revised edition (New Haven and London, 1971); Bernard Grofman and Arend Lijphart (eds) *Electoral Laws and Their Political Consequences* (New York, 1986). See also Nigel S. Roberts 'Proportional representation: lessons from abroad' and Robert M. Chapman 'On democracy as clear choice of government' in J. Stephen Hoadley (ed) *Improving New Zealand's Democracy* (Auckland, 1979) 73-84, 85-96; *Report of the Royal Commission on the Electoral System 'Towards a Better Democracy'* (Wellington, 1986) Ch. 2. For Social Credit support as protest voting, see David McCraw 'Social Credit's role in the New Zealand party system' *Political Science* 31 (1979) 54-60.

P.94 *MPs and constituents.* For the social and educational background of those who write to MPs, see Nigel S. Roberts 'Political letter writing and petition signing in New Zealand: a preliminary report' *New Zealand Journal of Public Administration* 37(1974) 35-42. For MPs' allocation of time, see Geoffrey Palmer *Unbridled Power* (Auckland, 1987) 104-7; J. Theodore Anagnoson, 'Home style in New Zealand' *Legislative Studies Quarterly* 8 (1983) 157-75.

P.97 *Representation*. For an account of representation and its different senses, see A. H. Birch *Representation* (London, 1972).

P.98 *Candidate selection*. See Keith Jackson *The Dilemma of Parliament* (Wellington, 1987) Ch. 4.

P.100 *Referendum*. See *Report of the Royal Commission on the Electoral System 'Towards a Better Democracy'* (Wellington, 1986) Ch. 7.

P.100 *Abortion*. For the effect of candidates' stands on abortion on performance at the polls, see Howard R. Penniman (ed) *New Zealand at the Polls* (Washington, 1980) 207-8, 240-1.

Chapter Four

P.103 *Interest groups*. For a general account of interest groups in New Zealand see Les Cleveland *The Anatomy of Influence* (Wellington, 1972). See also H. Gold, *New Zealand Politics in Perspective* (Auckland, 1985) Chs 19-21.

P.104 *Corporatism*. The concept of corporatism has been used in a number of different ways; see Peter J. Williamson *Varieties of Corporatism* (Cambridge, 1985). The account of corporatism closely follows that of Philippe C. Schmitter 'Still the century of corporatism' *Review of Politics* 36 (1974) 85-131, reprinted in Fredrick B. Pike and Thomas Stritch (eds) *The New Corporatism* (Notre Dame and London, 1974) 85-131. See also William A. Kelso *American Democratic Theory* (Westport and London, 1978) Ch. 2. For criticism of the analysis of corporatism given here, see N. Perry 'Review essay: corporatism tendencies in context' *Australia and New Zealand Journal of Sociology* 23 (1987) 117-20.

P.105 *Statutory bodies*. For an account of statutory bodies, see D. R. Hutton *The Role of Statutory Bodies in New Zealand Public Administration* Public Sector Research Papers 1.1 (1979). See also Geoffrey Palmer *Unbridled Power* (Auckland, 1987) Ch. 6; R. C. Mascarenhas 'Quasi-governmental bodies in New Zealand' *Public Sector* 7 (1984) 2-12.

P.107 *Federated Farmers*. For an account of the structure of Federated Farmers, see J. W. Talbot 'Federated Farmers of New Zealand' *Political Science* 23 (1971) 58-66, reprinted in Les Cleveland *The Anatomy of Influence* (Wellington, 1972) 83-91.

P.112 *Agricultural groups and parliament*. Evidence for the relations of various agricultural councils, boards and committees with parliament is taken from parliamentary debates. For examples from other sectors of government, see Frank Willie 'Pressure groups and parliamentary committees' in Les Cleveland *The Anatomy of Influence* (Wellington, 1972) 98-112.

P.115 *Wool acquisition*. The conflict over the proposal for compulsory acquisition of wool is described by Mary Ensor 'The agricultural sector in action: the quest for wool marketing reform, 1964-1972' in Stephen Levine (ed) *Politics in New Zealand* (Sydney, 1978), 321-332.

P.121 *Educational interest groups*. For the major teachers' organizations, see S. J. Ingle 'A comparative study of two educational pressure groups' in Les

Cleveland *The Anatomy of Influence* (Wellington, 1972) 41-54; see also Margaret Clark (ed) *The Politics of Education in New Zealand* (Wellington, 1981).

P.121 *Deregulation.* For state owned enterprises, see John Roberts *Public Servants and Public Enterprise* (Wellington, 1987) Chs 6-7; Bob Gregory 'The reorganisation of the public sector: the quest for efficiency' in Jonathan Boston and Martin Holland (eds) *The Fourth Labour Government* (Auckland, 1987). For the Business Roundtable, see Jack Vowles 'Business and Labour: major organised interests in the political economy of New Zealand' in H. Gold (ed) *New Zealand Politics in Perspective* (Auckland, 1985) 226; articles in *New Zealand Listener* 6 December 1986, 16 April 1988, *Sunday Star* 20 December 1987.

P.125 *Interests and classes.* The class bias of interest group activity is well documented in most modern representative democracies. The classic critique of interest group democracy, referring to the United States, is E. E. Schattschneider *The Semisovereign People* (New York, 1960). See also L. J. Sharpe 'American democracy reconsidered', part 1, *British Journal of Political Science* 3 (1973) 1-28.

P.128 *CARP.* See Christine Williams 'New Zealand cause groups: pressure politics and political "success" ' in Stephen Levine (ed) *Politics in New Zealand* (Sydney, 1978) 301-9.

Chapter Five

P.134 *Local government in New Zealand.* This chapter has drawn heavily on Graham W. A. Bush *Local Government and Politics in New Zealand* (Sydney, 1980). See also G. A. Wood *Governing New Zealand* (Auckland, forthcoming 1988) Chs 9-10.

P.135 *Labour's reforms.* For an account of local body reform in the 1970s, see Mary A. Ronnie and P. S. O'Connor 'Local government' in Ian Wards (ed) *Thirteen Facets* (Wellington, 1978) 133-166.

P.136 *Local elections.* See John Halligan and Paul Harris 'Local elections and democracy' in Stephen Levine (ed) *Politics in New Zealand* (Sydney, 1978) 241-254; Paul Harris and John Halligan 'Local government elections in New Zealand' *Politics* 12 (1977) 143-147; Paul Harris 'Patterns of party support in Wellington City local body elections, 1974 and 1977' *Political Science* 33 (1981) 33-51.

P.138 *Duty to vote.* The borough surveyed was Gisborne. See Women's Electoral Lobby (Gisborne) *Local Body Survey*, 1977 cited by Graham W. A. Bush *Local Government and Politics in New Zealand* (Sydney, 1980) 200.

P.139 *Party in local politics.* For the relative absence of party competition in local government, see Geoffrey Debnam 'Tradition and change in New Zealand local government' *Journal of Commonwealth and Comparative Politics* 17 (1979) 300-315.

P.144 *Social background of candidates.* See John Halligan and Paul Harris 'Local elections and democracy' in Stephen Levine (ed) *Politics in New Zealand* (Sydney, 1978) 241-254.

P.147 *Community councils.* See G. A. Wood 'New Zealand's community councils in the 1970s' *Political Science* 31 (1979) 1-17.

P.152 *Apathy in local government.* See Robert Gregory 'Political participation in New Zealand: the democratic idea in local government reform' in Stephen Levine (ed) *Politics in New Zealand* (Sydney, 1978) 50-62.

P.156 *'Integrative' function.* See Geoffrey Debnam 'Tradition and change in New Zealand local government' *Journal of Commonwealth and Comparative Politics* 17 (1979) 300-315; see also Jane J. Mansbridge *Beyond Adversary Democracy* (New York, 1980).

Chapter Six

P.164 *Justification of democracy.* Classic defences of democratic government are J. J. Rousseau *The Social Contract* (1762) and J. S. Mill *Considerations on Representative Government* (1861). Useful modern discussions are Henry B. Mayo *An Introduction to Democratic Theory* (New York, 1960) Chs 9-10; Carl Cohen *Democracy* (Athens, Georgia, 1971) Chs 14-16; Jack Lively *Democracy* (Oxford, 1975) Ch. 4; William N. Nelson *On Justifying Democracy* (London, 1980) Ch. 3. For the educative value of participation see Carole Pateman *Participation and Democratic Theory* (Cambridge, 1970); J. Roland Pennock and John W. Chapman (eds) *Participation in Politics* (New York, 1975).

Index